Warsaw is My Country

The Story of Krystyna Bierzyńska, 1928–1945

Jews of Poland

Series Editor
ANTONY POLONSKY (Brandeis University)

Warsaw is My Country

The Story of
Krystyna Bierzyńska,
1928–1945

BETH
HOLMGREN

Boston
2018

Library of Congress Cataloging-in-Publication Data:

The bibliographic data for this title is available from the Library of Congress.

©Academic Studies Press, 2018
ISBN 978-1-61811-758-8 (hardback)
ISBN 978-1-61811-759-5 (paperback)
ISBN 978-1-61811-760-1 (electronic)

Book design by Kryon Publishing Services (P) Ltd.
www.kryonpublishing.com

Cover design by Ivan Grave

Published by Academic Studies Press
28 Montfern Avenue
Brighton, MA 02135, USA
press@academicstudiespress.com
www.academicstudiespress.com

Contents

Dedication	vi
Acknowledgments	vii
List of Illustrations	viii
Introduction	x
1 Under the Portrait of Gustawa	1
2 Being a Bierzyński	6
3 Warsaw before the War, 1928–1939	12
4 A Citizen of the World	20
5 Warsaw: Invasion and Occupation, 1939–1940	26
6 Learning the Life of a Fugitive, 1940–1942	37
7 Warsaw: A Conspiratorial Identity, 1942–1944	49
8 The 1944 Warsaw Uprising	68
9 A Polish Prisoner of War, 1944–1945	84
10 A Family Pact	95
11 Krystyna Bierzyńska in Polish History	107
Works Cited	111
Index	113

Dedicated with gratitude and love to Krystyna Bierzyńska Stamper, and in memory of her parents Beniamin and Stefania and brother Adolf.

Acknowledgments

My greatest thanks go to Krystyna Bierzyńska Stamper for her generosity, patience, time, effort, and willingness to share both information and contacts as I familiarized myself with her story, family, and life in Poland. You are my beloved hero, Krystyna! I am awed by your capacity for friendship, indefatigable drive to do the right thing, and super sense of humor.

I thank Krystyna and Jim Stamper for their gracious hospitality during my visits to Newport Beach, California. I am grateful to Grażyna Stęcka and Eve Chapman for the information they provided me about the extended Bierzyński-Stęcki families.

I am indebted to my two readers at Academic Studies Press for their astute queries, criticisms, and suggestions. Their feedback greatly improved the manuscript. The mistakes remaining are mine. Thanks also to the colleagues who responded to my questions about life and death in interwar and wartime Poland—Madeline G. Levine, Antony Polonsky, Karen Auerbach, Magdalena Kozłowska, and Sean Martin.

I am grateful to the staff at Academic Studies Press who handled the review, editing, and production process of *Warsaw Is My Country* so well—Faith Wilson Stein, Matthew Charlton, Oleh Kotsyuba, and Kira Nemirovsky. Thanks also to the editors who worked with manuscript: Eileen Wolfberg and Suzanne Wertheim.

Travel costs for my trips to interview Krystyna Stamper were covered by a grant from the Josiah Charles Trent Memorial Foundation, an important donor for many worthy educational projects undertaken at Duke University.

Beth Holmgren
Chapel Hill, North Carolina

List of Illustrations

1. Portrait of Gustawa Landau Neufeld. From collection of Krystyna Bierzyńska Stamper.
2. Group photo of the Bierzyński family. From collection of Krystyna Bierzyńska Stamper.
3. Painting of Marshal Józef Piłsudski on his favorite horse, Kasztanka, Artist: Wojciech Kossak. 1928. In the public domain.
4. Marshal Piłsudski reviewing the infantry division during the commemoration of Independence Day (November 11, 1926) on Piłsudski Square. From Narodowe Archiwum Cyfrowe. I-P-2943-9.
5. The Summer Theater in 1871 in the Saxon Gardens. Photographer: Konrad Brandel, December 31, 1870. In the public domain.
6. Saxon Gardens. Slide in front of the water tower, 1927. From Narodowe Archiwum Cyfrowe. I-U-7362-3.
7. The Royal Palace in Warsaw in flames following German bombardment, September 17, 1939. Photographer: Unknown. In the public domain.
8. Headstone for the graves of Bronisław (Beniamin) Bierzyński, Stefania Bierzyńska, and Regina Bierzyńska in the old Zabierzów Cemetery. Photo by author.
9. From left: Marysia Bierzyńska (Krystyna's cousin, Henryk and Rega's daughter), Krystyna, and unknown man. Zabierzów. Taken between 1940 and 1942. From collection of Krystyna Bierzyńska Stamper.
10. Krystyna's Aunt Nina and her family: from left, Wanda Warszawska (daughter), Dr. Fabian Warszawski, and Dr. Janina (Nina) Warszawska. From collection of Krystyna Bierzyńska Stamper.
11. Wartime photo of Basia Raczkowska. From collection of Krystyna Bierzyńska Stamper.
12. Wartime photo of Stefan Zacieniuk. From collection of Krystyna Bierzyńska Stamper.

13. Dr. Janina Marczewska and her daughter in later years. Seated bottom left: Dr. Janina Marczewska. Standing from left to right: Grażyna Stęcka (Krystyna's cousin, granddaughter of Matylda Bierzyńska Stęcka): Monika Marczewska, and Dr. Marysia Marczewska (daughter of Janina Marczewska). From collection of Krystyna Bierzyńska Stamper.
14. German destruction of housing block at the intersection of Zamenhof and Wołyńska Streets in the Warsaw Ghetto during the Ghetto Uprising. Author unknown. In the public domain.
15. Krystyna and Basia Raczkowska in Świder in the summer of 1944. From collection of Krystyna Bierzyńska Stamper.
16. Krystyna relaxing in Świder in the summer of 1944. From collection of Krystyna Bierzyńska Stamper.
17. Street barricades constructed during the 1944 Warsaw Uprising at the intersection of Żytnia and Karolkowa Streets. Photographer: Stefan Bałuk. August 1, 1944. In the public domain.
18. Patrol of Home Army female orderlies on Moniuszko Street. Photographer: Eugeniusz Lokajski. August 5, 1944. In the public domain.
19. Units of the Home Army leave Warsaw after capitulating to the Germans. October 1944. From Narodowe Archiwum Cyfrowe. 21-223.
20. Photo of "Krystyna the Blue" in the uniform made for her at Sandbostel. From collection of Krystyna Bierzyńska Stamper; appears here as reproduced for the "Insurgents' Biographies" archived in the Museum of the Warsaw Uprising.
21. The liberation of Oberlangen by Polish forces. Narodowe Archiwum Cyfrowe, sygn. 37-339-1.
22. Photocopy of envelope from Professor Gergovich to Krystyna. From collection of Krystyna Bierzyńska Stamper.
23. Photocopy of letter from Professor Gergovich to Krystyna. First page. From the collection of Krystyna Bierzyńska Stamper.
24. Photocopy of letter from Professor Gergovich to Krystyna. Second page. From the collection of Krystyna Bierzyńska Stamper.
25. Dr. Adolf (Dolek) Bierzyński in uniform of the Polish II Corps. From collection of Krystyna Bierzyńska Stamper.
26. Photo of Dolek and Krystyna taken several decades after the war. From collection of Krystyna Bierzyńska Stamper.
27. Group photo of Krystyna Bierzyńska Stamper and James Stamper (seated in front row) surrounded by family members and friends. From collection of Krystyna Bierzyńska Stamper.

Introduction

In October 2008, I first met Krystyna Bierzyńska (Bye-ZHIN-ska) Stamper in Santa Ana, California. I had flown out from my home in North Carolina, where I teach Polish and Russian literatures and cultures at Duke University, to give a lecture on Helena Modjeska (1840–1909), a great Polish and American actress who had built her star home, called "Arden," in the inland wilderness of Orange County, California, in the 1880s. Krystyna, an attractive, vigorous woman in her seventies, was one of the founding members of the Helena Modjeska Foundation, a nonprofit dedicated to preserving the actress's California home and legacy. She had volunteered to drive me from my Santa Ana hotel to Modjeska's "Arden." As I soon learned, helping maintain this site of Polish American heritage for visitors and special delegations was the sort of dedicated service that came naturally to Krystyna.

As we swapped stories about ourselves during that drive from the coast into the countryside, I learned that long before Krystyna Bierzyńska had married James Stamper and settled in Newport Beach, California, she had fought in the 1944 Warsaw Uprising. I had met other Poles who had served as soldiers, orderlies, and couriers in this horrific sixty-three-day street-by-street battle between the David of the Polish Home Army and the Goliath of the German Reich. (In this version, alas, Goliath prevailed.) But I had never met someone who had been so young when the Uprising erupted. Krystyna had been just sixteen when the battle began and had thrown herself into the fray. After the battle's end, when the German army recognized her and over seventeen hundred other Polish women combatants as prisoners of war—a rare distinction given the Reich's treatment of most captured Poles as slaves or worse—she became one of the youngest inmates in the female POW camp that the Germans hastily outfitted at Oberlangen.

I wanted to know all the details of Krystyna's war story. What could be more inspiring, more thrilling, than the tale of an adolescent girl who takes up arms against the Nazis and survives as a much-commemorated veteran? I knew so many women, myself included, who longed to be that kind of girl, though it is doubtful many of us would have had the courage to do so.

Krystyna described her 1944 service as a foregone conclusion. Her parents were already dead, and her brother was off serving as a doctor in General Władysław Anders's Army, a 100,000-man force that fought alongside American and British Allies. (Krystyna always believed her brother was alive, and did not know until after the war that he had been wounded saving the lives of Polish soldiers during their hard-fought battles up the spiny boot of Italy.) Earlier, after her mother's arrest, Krystyna had left her relatives in the south and had returned to her hometown of Warsaw, where her beloved surrogate family, the close friends of her parents and relatives, conspired together to keep her safe and sound. By 1944, many Varsovians, most of them young, were champing at the bit to oust the hated German occupiers before the Soviet Army, under the leadership of Joseph Stalin, could "liberate" Warsaw on its own occupying terms.

By the end of my California visit in 2008, I was dying to hear more of Krystyna's story and urging her to share it. Krystyna was not yet sure she wanted to commit it to print. I begged her to call me if she changed her mind. In the meantime, I completed the cultural biography I was writing on Helena Modjeska and embarked on several other projects. I was delighted to meet Krystyna again in April 2012, when I returned to Santa Ana to give readings from my just-published Modjeska book. I did not pass up this opportunity to encourage Krystyna to write—if not with me, then with some other author. Finally, after multiple phone calls, Krystyna decided to work with me on her story in spring 2014, the year that marked the seventieth anniversary of the 1944 Warsaw Uprising. Before I committed, however, Krystyna requested that I review material that she had just mailed to me.

As it turned out, it was not only Krystyna's combat experience that was remarkable. As I learned from the material Krystyna had sent to me, a video of her interview with a Shoah volunteer, she was in fact an acculturated Jew who had survived the Holocaust through sheer good luck, personal moxie, and the combined efforts of her parents, friends, and unknown helpers. This born-and-bred Warsaw girl had been spirited out of the capital as the Nazis corralled Jews into their newly made Ghetto. Through her parents' foresight and quick action, Krystyna had survived the majority of the war mostly in plain sight in southern Polish towns, while her blonde-haired, blue-eyed mother traveled to the Częstochowa and Warsaw Ghettos to buy her relatives' freedom (or, when that was impossible, to provide them with food and other staples). After her mother's arrest, Krystyna returned alone to her native city, where that network of family friends helped keep her alive even as she prepared to fight for Warsaw's liberation.

The conscientious Shoah volunteer in Krystyna's video clearly did not realize just how exceptional Krystyna's experience was. I desperately wanted to project myself into the interviewer's seat, put Krystyna at ease, and ask her a thousand more questions. Even before I had finished watching the video, I was on the phone to Krystyna. We planned our first three-day marathon interviewing session in September 2014.

The interviewing process proved to be exhilarating, exhausting, and, once started, impossible to stop. It was as if Krystyna and I were trying to unearth a fragile artifact with endlessly branching parts. Krystyna was an excellent storyteller and I was an eager, if at first somewhat fumbling, questioner. After each recording session, we would start by going over what we had just discussed. As I transcribed the recordings at home in North Carolina, I'd call Krystyna with more requests for clarification. In return, she'd contact me as forgotten memories rose to the surface. By the time Krystyna and I plunged into a second interview marathon in October 2015, my interim research on the Warsaw that Krystyna had known, the memoirs of other Holocaust survivors, and histories of Poland and its Jewish citizens during World War II prompted me to ask questions I hadn't known I needed to ask before. During this session, we both worked at an accelerated rhythm and with much greater familiarity, often dissolving into laughter or tears. I believe that our question-and-answer exchange will continue the rest of our lives.

The result of our collaboration is this book, Krystyna Bierzyńska's story from her birth in Warsaw in 1928 up to the few months after the war's end in May 1945, when she was finally reunited with her brother, Dolek. This story defies categorization as either Holocaust or Warsaw Uprising memoir. It tells the tale of a remarkable young heroine and a diverse supporting cast of extraordinary individuals—Polish Jews, Polish Catholics, and at least one Russian. It is also a Warsaw story, a biography that demonstrates how in early twentieth-century Polish culture and society, being a liberal educated Pole and being an acculturated, but unconverted, Jew overlapped significantly. Krystyna's story tells us a great deal about the complicated identities, obstacles, and possibilities Jews encountered in interwar urban Poland. The acculturated children of Orthodox Jewish parents or grandparents—in this story, the parents of Krystyna's father —walked a fine line between an old-fashioned religious milieu they did not wish to endanger (but had no desire to inhabit) and a tantalizingly modern world of both obvious opportunities and lurking antisemitism. At the same time, the many acculturated Jews who were busy creating the culture and developing the economy and industries of independent Poland at last dared to believe that they qualified as Poles—as citizens and patriots whose differences in ethnicity and religious orientation would no longer stigmatize them.

Krystyna's story details a Jewish girl's remarkable experience of three very different Polands: a cosmopolitan oasis of high culture, modern amenities, and tolerance engineered by her educated, affluent parents; a sequence of shabby provincial quarters pervaded by fear, loss, and hypervigilance as the Germans pursued all Jews as permissible prey; and an occupied capital intoxicated and united by conspiracy, where the residents joined together to overthrow a common enemy. Warsaw was her defining, magnetic context. More than any other narrative that I have read or heard, Krystyna Bierzyńska's memories of her prewar childhood and wartime adolescence reveal the fascinating and infuriating complexities of what can constitute Polish Jewish identity.

I am indebted to Krystyna Bierzyńska for this extraordinary education. But I most treasure our collaboration because it allowed me to get to know, love, and unabashedly adore a wonderful, passionate, frank, funny, caring, sharp-witted, and fearless real-life heroine. Krystyna Bierzyńska's friendship has become one of the most precious relationships in my life.

CHAPTER 1

Under the Portrait of Gustawa

In 1967, after an absence of twenty-three years, Krystyna Bierzyńska felt compelled to return to Poland. When she had last seen her native country, her capital had lain in smoldering ruins, her Jewish relatives were dead or in hiding, and Nazi Germany had reinforced its vicious occupation of Poland in the wake of the 1944 Warsaw Uprising. Now thirty-nine years old, Krystyna was settled in the United States with a husband and two children, but she insisted on going back to Poland alone.

Her goal was to find photographs. She longed most for a picture of her mother, who had been arrested in Warsaw in 1943 and very likely had been murdered in the Nazi death camp of Treblinka. Krystyna also planned to visit her Polish "family," the friends who had loved her as a daughter and had helped her survive after her mother's disappearance. But she did not forewarn these friends about her impending arrival. The People's Republic of Poland in 1967 was alien, possibly dangerous, territory for her and any Polish citizens she might contact. The Moscow-allied Polish government kept track of visitors from the other side of the Iron Curtain. Besides, Krystyna wanted to experience the first hours of her return on her own.

Over the course of the two and a half weeks she spent in Poland, Krystyna grieved, wept, reconnected with loved ones, and carried out her search. She revisited the familiar Warsaw sights of her childhood, many of which had been rebuilt since the war. She rejoiced to see her friends, with whom she swapped stories of postwar experiences and news of family. And she hunted for photographs. Krystyna first searched in Warsaw, where her father had stored family property in his company's warehouse for safekeeping. She then continued her search in the small town of Zabierzów, near Kraków, where she, her parents, and her paternal uncle's family had taken refuge in the first years of the war, before the Germans had begun rounding up Jews.

But all of her family's belongings had vanished. They had disappeared under the rubble of Warsaw, had been sold by those entrusted to take care of them, or had been destroyed by former landlords who feared Nazi reprisal if it was discovered that they had been harboring Jews. During the war, the Nazi penalty for any Pole aiding a Jew had been execution.

Just before Krystyna finished her trip, she paid a final visit to one branch of her "Polish" family, Dr. Janina Marczewska and her grown daughter Maria in Warsaw. In dental school, Doctor Marczewska had become fast friends with Krystyna's youngest maternal aunt, Janina (Nina) Warszawska, and that friendship had extended to other members of Nina's family. When Krystyna had traveled alone to Warsaw in 1942, searching for her mother and fleeing the ever more frequent Nazi roundups of Jews in southern Poland, she had knocked first on Doctor Marczewska's door. From that moment on, young Krystyna's welfare had been the responsibility of a female triumvirate assembled by Marczewska. In 1967, when the adult Krystyna told Doctor Marczewska that her hunt for family photographs had turned up nothing, the elderly dentist wrought one more miracle. While she had not saved any photographs of Krystyna's mother, she was able to present Krystyna with a large photograph of an attractive, middle-aged woman gazing intently into the camera. The woman's high-collared dress and thick, dark hair piled up in a bun suggested that her portrait had been taken in the last decades of the nineteenth century.

Figure 1. Portrait of Gustawa Landau Neufeld. From collection of Krystyna Bierzyńska Stamper.

The photograph that Doctor Marczewska had managed to preserve was of Krystyna's mother's mother, Gustawa Neufeld (née Landau).

Krystyna knows very little about her maternal grandparents. Her grandfather Neufeld died young, leaving Gustawa widowed at an early age with three daughters to bring up and marry off. Gustawa herself had died years before Krystyna was born. Yet the vaguely remembered figure of Gustawa Neufeld is of immense importance to Krystyna's heritage and story. She not only engineered Krystyna's birth by matching her middle daughter, Stefania, with Krystyna's father, but she also forged her daughters' fates and Stefania's character through her ingenuity, adaptability, and pluck. Gustawa was her daughters' most astute and powerful role model. In testament to their love for her, all three of Gustawa's children—Aniela, Stefania, and Nina—hung her portrait above their beds in lieu of the usually matched portraits of father and mother. The copy that Doctor Marczewska gave Krystyna was from Nina's home. It was the one family memento that had survived the Warsaw Ghetto Uprising.

Gustawa Neufeld was most likely an educated, middle-class Jew, a woman familiar with big-city life and Polish sociocultural advantages. She and her daughters lived in Łódź, a city growing at breakneck speed in the latter half of the nineteenth century along with its burgeoning cotton industry. In this volatile "Polish Manchester," German and Jewish merchants made and lost fortunes overnight, while working-class Jews and Poles labored in its mills, which polluted the surroundings. The large Jewish community in Łódź included Hasidic and non-Hasidic Orthodox Jews, Zionists, Bundists, socialists, and modern secular Jews who often made common cause with an educated Polish Catholic intelligentsia.

It is unlikely that Gustawa was a religiously observant Jew. She wears no *sheytl* (Orthodox wig) in her photograph, and, if her daughters' behavior is any indication, she did not insist that they carry on Jewish religious traditions, observe Jewish holidays, or cook Jewish foods. Her children's Polish diction was flawless; Polish, not Yiddish, was probably the language they used at home. Based on the cultural and professional ambitions of Stefania and Nina, Gustawa had not raised her girls to become good Orthodox wives and mothers. Instead, her two younger daughters emulated modern, emancipated Polish women.

In one matter, however, Gustawa followed Jewish tradition for her daughters' material, if not spiritual, welfare. She moved the family from busy, sprawling Łódź, where the Jewish marriage market was most competitive, to the nearby, much smaller, and more manageable town of Tomaszów Mazowiecki. Here, Jewish industrialists and merchants thrived on a somewhat lesser scale: in the 1880s and 1890s, Jews made up between 40 and 50 percent of the population.[1] In Tomaszów Mazowiecki, the cost of living was lower and access to wealthy Jewish bachelors easier, and Gustawa was able to find the perfect husband for her oldest daughter, Aniela. Adolf Zylber was a blond-haired, blue-eyed acculturated Jew, a factory owner, and a consummate gentleman.

---

1 Information from webpages for Tomaszów Mazowiecki on Virtual Shtetl, http://www.sztetl.org.pl/en/article/tomaszow-mazowiecki/3,local-history, accessed January 3, 2017.

Adolf and Aniela adored each other all their lives, even after Adolf's fortune dwindled. Zylber was also a generous brother-in-law for Stefania and Nina. While he was still well-to-do, he sponsored both young women as they pursued their modern dreams. The artistic middle daughter, Stefania, gravitated to Kraków, where she worked in a photographer's studio retouching negatives and studied for some time in the city's esteemed Academy of Fine Art. Nina likely depended on Adolf to finance her degree in dentistry. Nina also found a good husband: she married Fabian Warszawski, a doctor specializing in dermatology. The two of them lived and worked as a professional couple, sharing contiguous offices in the same building where they had their apartment.

Once Stefania had tested and abandoned the dream of becoming an artist, Gustawa arranged for her marriage in 1912 to an up-and-coming young merchant, Beniamin Bierzyński. It was an auspicious match of two highly intelligent people, if not the serene idyll of Aniela and Adolf's union, and Gustawa had found Stefania an ambitious and forward-looking provider.

Benio, as his family called him, had no intention of limiting his life and work to what was on offer in small-time Tomaszów Mazowiecki. By 1918, he and Stefania had moved north to Warsaw, Poland's grandest and most cosmopolitan city. Here, Benio's business in the fur trade prospered and Krystyna was born. Krystyna's older brother Adolf, nicknamed Dolek, had been born in Tomaszów Mazowiecki four years before the Bierzyńskis resettled in the capital. Though very different in temperament and behavior, Stefania and Benio lived together in relative harmony. Stefania often deferred to her flamboyant husband, but instilled her values in her children and ran the household with a sure, kind hand. As the war years revealed in full, Stefania had inherited her mother's resourcefulness and courage.

Krystyna knows nothing more about her grandmother. But she was glad and grateful to receive Gustawa's portrait. Krystyna has accorded it a place of pride in her Newport Beach home, where it hangs as both welcome and blessing next to the front door. Gustawa's knowing eyes looked on as Krystyna and I delved into her past for this biography. During those interviews, it struck me that Gustawa would approve of her surviving granddaughter as a kindred spirit. Krystyna had been a resilient young woman who literally moved on after her father's death and her mother's disappearance, braving the return to her hometown. Krystyna survived and created a life for herself in spite of the successive challenges of the Holocaust, the 1944 Warsaw Uprising, seven months as a prisoner of war, and permanent displacement. In so doing, she demonstrated the strength and adaptability of her mother and her mother's mother before her.

Gustawa, moreover, would likely have tolerated the coexistence of Krystyna's Jewish heritage and strong Catholic faith. As an acculturated Jew, a widowed and anxious single parent of three daughters, and a mother revered by those daughters, be they cultivated wives or licensed dentists, Gustawa Neufeld was the grandparent best equipped to accept what worked, to appreciate the complex needs of Krystyna's worldly, war-torn life. If anyone could qualify as Krystyna's pragmatic guardian angel, it was Gustawa Landau Neufeld.

CHAPTER 2

Being a Bierzyński

Figure 2. Group photo of the Bierzyński family. From collection of Krystyna Bierzyńska Stamper.

Krystyna returned home from Poland in 1967 with the unexpected treasure of her grandmother's portrait, but never gave up her quest for more family photos. Her mother's missing image haunted her most. She also hoped that her mother's albums, filled with pictures of her and Dolek as children, had survived somewhere, somehow. Krystyna did not want to believe that a former landlord had burned all these memories as "incriminating evidence" of his kindness to her Jewish family.

The one photo of her mother that Krystyna did eventually recover literally appeared on her doorstep. In 1972, Krystyna's cousin Henryk, the son of her paternal uncle Bernard, came to visit the United States and presented her with a copy of a Bierzyński family portrait. The photo depicts two generations of Bierzyńskis, divided into standing and seated tiers, posed somberly around a small table. Krystyna's mother, Stefania, is on the far right, behind her seated husband, with one hand placed on his arm as if to mark possession. Stefania looks lovely and wary, haloed by her wavy blonde hair, not at all resembling the older mother Krystyna remembers. She is a young, aloof-seeming woman outnumbered by the strong dark clan of the Bierzyńskis.

In contrast to Gustawa Neufeld's three daughters, all of whom married well, paid little attention to their Jewish heritage, and lived the sort of lives that they themselves improvised, the Bierzyńskis were more connected to Jewish religious and cultural traditions and strongly influenced by maternal rules. Benio's parents, Natan and Berta (née Warmbrünn), were observant Jews who had settled in the provincial town of Koło, where they raised four children: Matylda, the eldest and the only daughter, and three sons, Beniamin, Bernard, and Henryk. Natan was a grain merchant who earned his family a good living and traveled as far as the European capital of Vienna on business. Berta, a German Jew with a penchant for cleanliness, order, frugality, and fresh air, believed in strict discipline and rugged physical conditioning (a belief that apparently stemmed from her temperament, not her piety). A strong-willed woman who ruled over both servants and children, Berta ordered her maid to wash the windows each day in a relentless battle with dust. In the winter, she insisted that the dustless windows be kept wide open and her boys not given hot water bottles at bedtime. She wanted to make sure that her children were not made soft by the comforts that Natan's money could give them.

Family history, on careful display in the photo, shows the Bierzyńskis already acculturating in Natan and Berta's generation. The Bierzyński men do not wear the long beards typical of traditional Orthodox Jews. Instead, three sport well-trimmed mustaches, conforming to the secular fashions of the modern world. None of the women, including the rule-obsessed Berta, cover their luxurious hair with a *sheytl*.

Though the photo is clearly staged to serve as a portrait of the family Bierzyński, the husband of the eldest child, Matylda, is not in the frame, and Matylda herself poses differently from the others, expressing diffidence or irritation, her elbows on the table and forearms raised and bared. Krystyna filled me in on the mystery of the missing husband. Apparently Benio had quarreled with Matylda's spouse, Henryk Stęcki, just before the photographer's visit and had laid down an ultimatum about who would and would not be in the picture. Benio sits on the far right, as if guarding the family gate.

The family's surname also indicates a Jewish clan in transition. Natan had seen to it that their original surname, Bieżuner, which looked and sounded

Jewish to Polish Gentiles, was polonized as Bierzyński, the "ż" replaced with the more traditional Polish consonant cluster "rz" (both "ż" and "rz" are pronounced "zh"), and the suffix "er" dropped for the quintessential Polish "ski," a marker of gentry status. The Polish language facility of the Bierzyński children indicates that Natan and Berta spoke Polish as a first or a second language at home. In addition, Berta, proud of her German origins, taught Benio how to read and write in that language. The letters that she and Benio exchanged once he moved to Warsaw were written in German, in a Gothic cursive.

Though the Bierzyński children remained attached to their parents and to each other, they scattered in their choices of profession, location, and lifestyle. All four came of age around World War I, which brought them both hardship and opportunity. Benio and Bernard continued in trade, but not in their father's footsteps. They both went into the fur business, importing skins from Scandinavia to Danzig to be cured and selling the finished furs as luxury items for Poland's growing middle class, which included both Jews and Christians. The Bierzyńskis' youngest, Henryk, took the most ambitious professional step, completing his medical degree. His education was funded by a generous Benio, just as Nina Neufeld's dental school bills were paid by her generous brother-in-law, Adolf Zylber. As a doctor, Henryk and his family qualified as educated professionals, members of their small-town intelligentsia.

The boldest changes that Natan and Berta's children ventured involved relocation, moving into a heterogeneous Polish world populated by Jews and Catholics, manual laborers and aristocrats, educated professionals and business owners big and small. The devilishly handsome Henryk, married to the chic Regina, moved to the town of Zabierzów, which was not far from the picturesque old Polish capital of Kraków and quite remote from the mill towns that fueled his father's and brothers' fortunes. There, Henryk quickly established himself as the preferred doctor for local landowning aristocrats, who hired him to care for their many workers. Henryk came to know one branch of the fabulously wealthy Radziwiłł family, who once owned twenty-three palaces, over four hundred towns, and two thousand estates.

Henryk's relationship with the august Radziwiłłs allowed him to obtain a purebred Radziwiłł dachshund for his niece Krystyna. Named Żabka (Froggy) because of the shape of her legs, this dachshund was utterly spoiled by her new family, and was dressed on wintry days in a grey shearling coat with green wool backing, courtesy of B. Bierzyński and Company. Indeed, Żabka had landed in the Bierzyński family's most opulent home, and was the pet of the son who had achieved the greatest financial and social success. Benio risked and won the most in his career, moving his wife, family, and fur business out of Tomaszów Mazowiecki to Warsaw. Dolek's earliest memories of the capital are of the unprepossessing apartment the family rented on Żurawia Street. But by the time Krystyna was born in 1928, fourteen years after Dolek, her family was more than comfortably settled in a huge second-floor apartment at 1 Piłsudski Square, the swanky heart of the city.

In the early 1920s, Warsaw offered enterprising acculturated Jews in Poland the greatest economic opportunities and lifestyle choices. A third of its residents were Jewish, ranging from insular Yiddish-speaking Hasidim to those who identified themselves as Polish through their choice of language, culture, and associations, if not by conversion to Christianity.[1] Benio strived to ensconce his family in Warsaw's highest attainable socioeconomic stratum, where all antisemitic prejudices presumably would melt away under the influence of wealth, urbanity, and shared good taste.

What did it mean, then, for Krystyna to be a Bierzyński? The family line with which she was familiar stretched from provincial Koło to the dazzling capital. Along that line lived her Uncle Bernard and his family, observant Jews who, as Krystyna recalls, "counted their pennies" in Tomaszów Mazowiecki; well-educated and secular Uncle Henryk and his wife and two children, who led the life of a respected doctor's family in a town close to Kraków; and her acculturated, upper-class parents, who loved their new hometown, albeit for different reasons. During childhood, Krystyna also knew her paternal grandparents, though not in the context of their provincial home. Natan visited her family in Warsaw on his way back from Vienna when she was five, making his stay memorable with the gift of an elaborately detailed miniature store that was painted pink. Berta, renowned for her high standards of cleanliness, also visited 1 Piłsudski Square, putting everyone in the household on their mettle. Krystyna recalls Berta most vividly, however, when her grandmother helped Stefania nurse a terminally ill Benio during the war, a strong-willed woman devoted to her family's welfare.

Krystyna did not associate her Bierzyński identity with Judaism— neither with Jewish spirituality nor with daily rituals. When she once sneaked a peek at her grandfather wearing *tefillin* and *davening* (praying), she was terrified that

---

1 Katarzyna Person offers this description of Warsaw's diverse Jewish population in *Assimilated Jews in the Warsaw Ghetto, 1940–1943* (Syracuse: Syracuse University Press, 2014), 8: "Interwar Warsaw, with its Jewish population ranging between 320,000 and 370,000, was undoubtedly the European center of Jewish life. Even though the vast majority of its Jewish inhabitants remained traditional, Warsaw was also the most assimilated city in a newly independent Poland."

he was having a seizure until her mother assured her otherwise. During the lone Passover seder that her parents held in honor of her grandmother's visit to Warsaw, Krystyna, a self-professed "picky eater," wanted nothing to do with the strange-tasting food.

Writer Joanna Olczak-Ronikier, whose grandfather Jakub Mortkowicz was a famous publisher of Polish literature, argues that ambitious Jewish assimilation entailed shame and pain:

> There is no need to hide the fact that, among Jews who had decided to assimilate, a huge role was played by ambitions relating to the level of Polonisation they had achieved. Where the parents, through their looks, language, and religious customs were a reminder of the environment that the children had made such an effort to get out of, family love and loyalty were severely put to the test.[2]

In Krystyna's case, however, family love and loyalty never seemed to be at risk. Benio and Stefania conveyed no disrespect towards Benio's parents, and Benio's parents took great pride in their son's success without any self-abasement. Krystyna's memories of the relationship between her parents and paternal grandparents intimate a strong emotional bond, as well as a shared drive to do well in worldly terms. The already acculturating Natan and Berta did not press their children to remain observant Jews or to pursue any identity, religious or political, that would sequester them from the mainstream of Polish society. Their children were to be cultured middle-class Europeans, not Zionists or socialists. Berta taught her children German, not Yiddish. Natan trailblazed larger European trade routes for his business-minded sons.

Krystyna told me that she always somehow knew that she was Jewish, though the contents of that Jewishness were never spelled out. She was much more profoundly aware that she was a Bierzyński. And she was lucky enough to share and discuss that awareness after the war with her brother and surviving first cousins. To a great extent, family identity eclipsed religious and ethnic identity for this generation, rendering any other shared connection, practice, or feature implicit. Krystyna and other family members of her generation liked to declare that a Bierzyński was "a hothead," "an extrovert" who verged on the bombastic, though they said this with a touch of pride in their hotheaded

---

2 Joanna Olczak-Ronikier, *In the Garden of Memory: A Family Memoir*, trans. Antonia Lloyd-Jones (London: Phoenix, 2005), 76.

parents' equally characteristic intelligence and self-confidence. If you were a Bierzyński, you always had an opinion and you always got things done.

For Krystyna and Dolek, Benio represented the most polished, expansive, big city edition of the Bierzyński type. In Warsaw, her father had found himself just the right incubator for his business acumen, social energy, and conspicuous consumption. Indeed, Warsaw's cosmopolitanism and incredible array of cultural and commercial amenities fundamentally shaped every member of Krystyna's immediate family. To Benio, Stefania, Dolek, and Krystyna, being a Bierzyński (by blood or marriage) automatically meant being a proud and progressive Varsovian.

CHAPTER 3

Warsaw before the War, 1928–1939

During one of our last interviews, Krystyna interrupted a wartime story with a kind of pledge of allegiance: "Warsaw I identify with my country. Warsaw is my country." When I pressed her about what she meant, she drew a careful distinction between "country" and "home." While the United States, the place where she had chosen to settle forever after, is now her home, she noted:

> But when someone asks me where are you from, the first thing I say is that I'm from Warsaw, Poland. That's how I answer. There would be no Poland without Warsaw to me. I mean, I love the country, but Warsaw . . . I love the city. I do to this day, even though it's different and things have gone. I think there is a spirit there that may not be in other parts of the country, and I may sound very provincial, but I think there was probably more heroism there than in other places in Poland. I'm sure I stand to be corrected, but that's how I feel. You know what they say about Varsovians.

I know very well what Poles outside of the capital say about Varsovians—that they are rascals, operators, braggarts, and parochial in the way that New Yorkers tend to be, convinced that their city is the center of the universe. Krystyna is none of the above. But she is a Varsovian born and bred, and she was born in "this country" of Warsaw at a moment when both its fortunes and her family's fortunes were ascendant.

Krystyna was the last of three children born to Stefania and Benio Bierzyński, and her birth came as something of a surprise. Her parents' first child, a son, was stillborn in 1912, a year after their wedding. Dolek, born on September 7, 1914, was a handsome and talented boy who seemed destined to be their only child. Fourteen years later, however, Krystyna made her grand entrance. She credits her birth to her brother's temporary bad luck and her own tenacity, her first victory in a lifelong sparring contest between siblings. When Stefania accompanied Dolek to Switzerland for a skiing trip in 1927, she surely did not know that she was pregnant. After Dolek crashed into a tree and broke his leg on the slopes, he required lengthy treatment at a Viennese hospital. By the time mother and son could return home, it was too late for Stefania to terminate the pregnancy, despite her advanced age of forty-one.

Krystyna was born on May 29, 1928, in a first-rate facility, Warsaw's Omega Maternity Hospital, located near the city center at 57 Aleje Jerozolimskie. The Bierzyńskis could afford the best of care for mother and child. Nonetheless, the birth of a ten-pound baby girl left her family a little shell-shocked. Stefania suffered from postpartum thrombosis and was consigned to bed with one swollen leg in a cast. A fleet of wet nurses and nannies tended Krystyna during her mother's convalescence. In the meantime, Dolek started teasing his baby sister long before she could retaliate. After Benio forced him to take a peek at the newborn Krystyna in the hospital nursery, Dolek voiced his disappointment without missing a beat: "I'd still rather have a monkey."

Regardless of Dolek's preferences, Krystyna came home to 1 Piłsudski Square, the carefully cocooned daughter of her middle-aged parents. Upper-class privilege and an indulgent family cushioned her initial bond with her hometown. The Bierzyńskis' address was impressively chic. Their imposing apartment building boasted a wide marble staircase, a wrought iron gate facing the square, and a clear prospect on the capital's grandest open space. Warsaw lay literally at Krystyna's tiny feet. Piłsudski Square was dedicated to Benio Bierzyński's still-living political idol, the charismatic Marshal Józef Piłsudski (1867–1935). Piłsudski began his political career as a socialist, led the fledgling Second Republic of Poland (1918–1939) to victory against the Soviet army in 1920, and forcibly guaranteed a pluralist Poland by staging a coup d'état against a right-wing nationalist government in 1926. In contrast to the right-wing, antisemitic National Democrats or Endecja, Piłsudski stood for religious and ethnic tolerance until his death in 1935. Benio, like many other young Jewish men who aspired to be patriots of a new Poland, had followed in Piłsudski's early footsteps during World War I, joining the future marshal's socialist faction and serving some time in prison for his political beliefs.[1]

---

1 On the generally good relations between Piłsudski and Jewish leaders in the 1920s, see Antony Polonsky's *The Jews in Russia and Poland: A Short History* (Oxford: Littman Library of Jewish Civilization, 2013), 223. In her memoir, Joanna Olczak-Ronikier notes that her radical great uncle, Maksymilian Horwitz, was at first devoted to the charismatic socialist Piłsudski before Horwitz became a member of the Communist Party (2005, 57).

Figure 3. Painting of Marshal Józef Piłsudski on his favorite horse, Kasztanka. Artist: Wojciech Kossak. 1928. In the public domain.

Standing on the balcony off her parents' drawing room, Krystyna had select access to a national stage. She could watch the changing spectacles played out on the square—the assorted military and civilian parades, the procession of dignitaries laying wreaths at the recently erected Tomb of the Unknown Soldier, or the forest of Christmas trees for sale that suddenly sprang up in December. On Piłsudski Square, a very young Krystyna glimpsed the marshal himself riding on a chestnut horse resembling his beloved Kasztanka, as iconic an image for Polish citizens as George Washington crossing the Delaware is for Americans. Even when the square was empty, it hummed with the activities of the establishments enclosing it: the serious business conducted at the Military Courts and the Ministry of Foreign Affairs, the customers perusing the giant showroom of the Polish Fiat car company, and the guests dining al fresco at the luxurious Hotel Europejski.

Benio's business added to the bustling commercial landscape of the city. The office for the furrier B. Bierzyński and Company stood on 7 Miodowa Street, which was lined with eighteenth-century palaces

Figure 4. Marshal Piłsudski reviewing the infantry division during the commemoration of Independence Day (November 11, 1926) on Piłsudski Square. From Narodowe Archiwum Cyfrowe. I-P-2943-9.

and mansions. The warehouse for his goods lay on the other side of the Vistula River in the Praga district, where rents were cheaper and the neighborhoods rougher. By 1937, despite the rollercoaster of the Polish economy, Benio's business was flourishing to the extent that he opened a fur salon in the city, where he employed an attractive young woman to model coats for potential buyers. Everyone in the family, including the dachshund Żabka, sported custom-made Bierzyński fur coats. On those rare evenings when Benio and Stefania attended the Warsaw Opera, Stefania dutifully modeled Bierzyński furs and the diamonds that her husband had given her, jewelry normally left locked up in a safety deposit box.

The Bierzyńskis' apartment at 1 Piłsudski Square placed them in close proximity to Mazowiecka Street, where Krystyna's parents could indulge in their respective big-city passions. The Zachęta National Art Gallery on Mazowiecka was a constant temptation for the artistic, contemplative Stefania. She bundled up Krystyna to tour new exhibits from the time that her daughter could walk, whether or not the little girl felt like being immersed in high culture that day. Benio positively thrived on the high life of the capital and regularly met his friends for an espresso at the Ziemiańska Café on Mazowiecka, the favorite watering hole for Warsaw's literati and stars of the cabaret and motion pictures. On weekdays, Stefania and her older sister, Aniela, who had moved to Warsaw with her husband Adolf after his factory closed, might pick up Krystyna after school and go strolling and shopping along lively, fashionable Marszałkowska Street, lovingly recalled by cabaret artist Kazimierz Krukowski as the prewar capital's "heart, brain, eyes, and ears":

> It was a miniature version of New York's 42nd Street or London's West End and Fleet Street. It boasted six theaters—the Malicka Theater, Mignon, Stańczyk, Ananas (Pineapple), Sfinks, and Czarny Kot (The Black Cat). Ten movie houses. One of the first cinemas was located at 118 Marszałkowska. Along its span, the newspaper *Kurier poranny* (The Morning Courier) marked its northern end and The Press House its southern, with *Wiadomości literackie* (*Literary news*) in the center, and Bukata, the great printing house, located at its intersection with Wspólna Street. The northern part of Marszałkowska, extending from Świętokrzyska Street, was a window on the world.[2]

---

2 Kazimierz Krukowski, *Moja Warszawka* (Warsaw: Filmowa Agencja Wydawnicza, 1957), 27.

On Sundays, when their live-in maid, Stasia, took her day off, the Bierzyńskis often made do by dining at Lardelli's, a café renowned for its pastries, chocolates, and ice cream. Warsaw's Great Theater stood just to the north of Piłsudski Square, but Krystyna's parents, particularly Benio, preferred to go to the cinema at any of the half-dozen movie palaces within walking distance. Krystyna remembers seeing a Polish-dubbed version of Walt Disney's *Snow White and the Seven Dwarves* (1937), the first full-length animated feature film ever produced.

Interwar Warsaw was a city of parks and abundant greenery. The Saxon Gardens, located close to Piłsudski Square, extended from the back of the magnificent Saxon Palace. Its expansive grounds housed assorted statues of rococo and late-nineteenth-century vintage, a fountain, an ornamental lake, a glass conservatory for palm trees, a marble sundial, and the Summer Theater, built entirely of wood with seating capacity for a little over a thousand patrons. Stefania once took Krystyna to a matinee performance of *A Midsummer Night's Dream* at the Summer Theater. In good weather, the Bierzyńskis visited the city's other natural playgrounds, picnicking at Paderewski Park or taking in the classical gardens, waterways, and palaces at Łazienki Park (the Royal Baths). They never purchased a car, unlike a growing number of well-to-do Varsovians who cruised the major thoroughfares in their bulky Packards and Buicks. Instead, the Bierzyńskis traveled by taxi or horse-drawn carriage. The latter form of transport, still popular in the 1930s, reflected a city very much

Figure 5. The Summer Theater in 1871 in the Saxon Gardens. Photographer: Konrad Brandel, December 31, 1870. In the public domain.

in the process of modernizing. When Warsaw was carpeted with snow, these old-fashioned conveyances became magical. Stefania, always sensitive to the picturesque, urged her daughter to listen for the sound of bells and be on the lookout for horse-drawn sleighs.

The Bierzyńskis represented new wealth in the interwar capital and partook of the city's many consumer pleasures. Yet they did not behave as nouveaux riches. Stefania incarnated decency, modesty, tranquility, and good taste at home. Despite her blonde hair, blue eyes, and hourglass figure, she avoided the spotlight of high society and disliked having to show off herself and her diamonds. Stefania did not smoke and almost never drank, with the exception of an occasional after-dinner liqueur. She most cherished the company of her family and close friends, books, and paintings. Krystyna remembers how her mother, a bit near-sighted, would read until dark and then savor what she called "the gray hour" of twilight, her favorite time of day. Stefania used the extravagant polar bear rug spread out on the floor of the Bierzyńskis' master bedroom as a reading lounge rather than a showpiece. She encouraged her children to do likewise. Rugs made out of real bear hides were popular among the rich and famous in the interwar decades, exotica tamed for domestic decoration. Stefania, Dolek, and Krystyna simply flopped down on the soft white fur and propped their books open on the bear's head.

Though Stefania eschewed smoking, drinking, and gallivanting, her training and sensibility as a visual artist inoculated her against prudery. In addition to her regular pilgrimages to the Zachęta Gallery, Stefania appropriated one wall of the drawing room for the exhibition of her own work. In this domestic gallery she included a portrait of a woman bared to the waist. When a curious Krystyna asked her about it, Stefania matter-of-factly described the portrait as a "half act," a term designating a semi-nude drawing of a human figure. Krystyna coolly repeated the term to the shocked little friends who visited her.

Stefania was most different from nouveau riche wives in her relationships with those who worked for her. She treated servants and outside hired help with deference and generosity. Stefania herself trained their indispensable maid, Stasia, to cook. When the washerwoman arrived to do the heavy cleaning, Stefania ceded her the kitchen for several days, all the while plying her with enormous slabs of bread piled with ham and repeating: "You must eat. You must eat well." This scene imprinted itself on Krystyna's memory: her mother's attending to the well-muscled laundress who reigned over vats of boiling clothes and a row of heavy irons.

Benio presented a very different role model. The pride of the Bierzyńskis, he relished center stage. Life as the owner of an established, flourishing business in the big city suited Benio down to the ground. A handsome, charming man, he was particular about the way he looked and dressed, as Krystyna delights in recalling:

> My father had these beautiful blue-gray eyes. He just wore the right things and said the right things and was a good businessman. My father was elegant. When he kissed me in the morning, I would tell him he smelled of cologne and coffee. His shoes were polished and his shirts were monogrammed.

Benio's polished shoes and monogrammed shirts intimated his general appetite for what Krystyna calls "the good stuff." In contrast to Stefania, who claimed just one wall for her past paintings, Benio was an avid, ostentatious collector who filled entire rooms with his purchases. And he had moved to a metropolis where he could consume on an expensive scale for show. Benio bought crystal wine goblets of every color and exquisite china coffee cups and saucers, transforming the drawing room into a showplace. The cups and saucers were laid out in a glass display case, resembling either fabulous works of art or the most expensive items in the store. The huge leather couches and the matching black Chippendale furniture that overwhelmed the rest of the room were Benio's idea, too, as was the black Blutner piano allotted one corner of the room and topped by a candelabra. This piece of beautiful furniture was meant for use as well, since Dolek proved to be a gifted pianist.

Benio's penchant for buying large quantities of top-of-the line goods may have reflected the impulsiveness his children attributed to the Bierzyński family. Yet he bought not to brag about his wealth, but to relish whatever caught his attention. Benio thought big, lived large, and enjoyed himself a great deal. Rather than investing in a complete set of leather-bound books to make his bookshelves look impressive, he instead selected intellectually adventurous volumes such as Maurice Maeterlinck's *The Life of the Bee* and *The Life of the Ant*, which he consumed from cover to cover and then secured in a locked bookcase. Benio was intrigued by new gadgets and new materials. After purchasing one of the first toasters sold in Warsaw, he enthusiastically demonstrated how it worked to his family at the dining room table, burning slices of bread in quick succession. On a shopping trip in Vienna, Benio snapped up some of the early products made of Bakelite to give to his wife, along with chocolates wrapped in tissue paper and packed in beautiful Viennese bonbonnieres.

Notwithstanding the great differences in their temperaments, Stefania and Benio remained together through the flush times and forged a strong united front during the early months of the war. They socialized well with each other's family members—Stefania with her exacting mother-in-law Berta and the family of Benio's favorite brother Henryk, and Benio with Stefania's older sister Aniela and her husband Adolf. Most importantly, Benio and Stefania developed friendships with Christians in the big, diverse city. Hybridity percolated in Warsaw's upper- and middle-class society through old school ties, professional associations, and shared living space. Doctor Marczewska, the former classmate of Stefania's sister Nina, became Krystyna's dentist and was a family friend for as long as Krystyna could remember. And the Bierzyńskis' neighbor in their building at 1 Piłsudski Square, Amelia Brzozowska, the wife and business partner of the famed Warsaw photographer Stanisław Brzozowski, became a very good friend indeed to Benio, Stefania, and Krystyna Bierzyński over the coming years.

Krystyna Bierzyńska thus spent her childhood in a beautiful, upscale Warsaw of gracious buildings, broad boulevards, lush parks, lavishly stocked stores, and every conceivable amenity. Her family seemed living proof that acculturated Jews with enough money and taste could make friends with liberal Christians and enjoy the same culture and leisure pastimes. Yet most of Warsaw remained a blank to the young Krystyna—its far-flung districts, middle-class and working-class neighborhoods, and highly varied Jewish communities, which ranged religiously from the Progressive to the Hasidim and politically from the Zionists to the Bundists. Krystyna would come to know her "country" best only when her parents' carefully circumscribed world was demolished by the war.

CHAPTER 4

A Citizen of the World

Upper-class privilege afforded young Krystyna the assorted delights of Lardelli's pastries, Bierzyński fur coats, afternoons spent reading with her gentle, perceptive mother, and outings with her elegant, worldly father. Yet, as Krystyna grew older, she began to chafe at the rich girl's cocoon her parents had constructed with such good intentions. Their reasons for protecting her were several. In comparison to Dolek, who had been a healthy child and a boy to boot, Krystyna suffered the double dangers of being a girl and sickly. In early childhood, she fell prey to one ailment after another—asthma, jaundice, colitis, bronchitis, and eczema. In addition, Krystyna, like her much older brother, was stigmatized by a condition nearly impossible to "treat." Though she could pass as a Gentile with her blonde hair and blue eyes, she was a Jew and therefore liable to be insulted or humiliated in any social environment that her parents could not control.

Whereas Dolek learned early to fend for himself, Benio and Stefania deemed Krystyna too fragile to socialize on her own. For example, she did not play with other children in her apartment building. Instead, her mother imported a sometime playmate from the cobbler's family who lived on the ground floor of 1 Piłsudski Square. High- and low-income Varsovians often resided in the same buildings, but only ground-floor rents were cheap enough for the working class. The cobbler's daughter was invited to the Bierzyńskis for an afternoon "tea" of hot cocoa and cakes with Krystyna. She behaved politely and gratefully, very likely according to her parents' instructions.

Krystyna's only other early companions were her governesses, who gave her lessons and escorted her out to play in the fresh air and tree-lined paths of the Saxon Gardens. Several governesses and at-home teachers stand out in Krystyna's memory. Her French instructors prepared her exceedingly well for school entrance examinations. Most intriguing was a young teacher named Genia, who made no secret of being Jewish and a Zionist. Krystyna loved Genia's stories of Jews in Mandate Palestine who grew oranges year-round and worked and lived in kibbutzim. Genia was the first Jew in Krystyna's experience who openly embraced her identity as distinctive and desirable.

Nevertheless, Stefania's careful vetting of playmates and governesses could not wholly protect Krystyna from antisemitic slights. While Krystyna cannot remember the incident that prompted a turning point in her young life, her brother Dolek remembered it for them both. One day, returning from an outing to the Saxon Gardens with one of her governesses, a tearful Krystyna rushed to her mother to find out why, in the words of some child, "Jewish girls were not allowed to play there." Her upset alarmed all three members of her family. Krystyna's cocoon, they realized, was penetrable. This galvanized them to find her the safest possible school.

Dolek, already in his early twenties, was most intent on readying his little sister for the world. Benio and Stefania had hoped that they could ensure an environment of tolerance and safety for their children through relocation to Warsaw, giving them the best education and using their affluence for social leverage. By the time Krystyna was school age, Dolek's bitter experience had proved them wrong, in large part because the multiethnic Poland initially promised by Piłsudski's leadership and coup d'état had lurched swiftly to the right. In the early 1930s, quotas that restricted the admission of Jewish students, the notorious numerus clausus, prevented Dolek from entering medical

Figure 6. Saxon Gardens. Slide in front of the water tower, 1927. From Narodowe Archiwum Cyfrowe. I-U-7362-3.

school in Warsaw. Like other frustrated Jewish parents of means, Benio hoped to circumvent Dolek's subseqent rejection from medical school in Kraków, Poland's other major academic center, with a substantial donation. Yet as soon as Benio thought he had secured Dolek's admission, the authorities chose to decry "Jewish bribery" in lieu of eliminating the unjust numerus clausus. It is no wonder that Dolek reacted so strongly to his little sister's tears. Just as Krystyna had been told that Jewish girls were not allowed to play in Polish parks, so he had faced a harsher, more substantive prohibition: qualified Jewish students were not allowed to study in Polish universities.

Benio ultimately coped with his son's problem by relocating him once again, this time moving him out of an increasingly nationalist Poland into France. Within a year of his arrival, Dolek began his medical training in France, studying first at provincial universities where he could improve his language skills until he was eventually admitted to the Sorbonne. There, Dolek chose the seemingly odd specialization of tropical medicine. He wrote his final thesis on the tsetse fly and its transmission of human and animal diseases. Krystyna remembers how Dolek dedicated this magnum opus in French: "pour ma mere et mon père et ma petite soeur."[1]

Benio considered himself a Polish patriot and a proud follower of Piłsudski, but he was a pragmatist where his family was concerned. In the late 1930s, Nazi Germany was swallowing up territories to its east without opposition from the west and was subjecting the Jews in those territories to the most virulent forms of persecution. If German expansion was not stopped, far worse was yet to come to Poland. In consequence, Benio and Stefania planned to move the entire family to France, selling their holdings in Warsaw and retreating to some peaceful spot on the French Riviera. Dolek was already establishing himself in France, so the Bierzyńskis only had to educate Krystyna toward this goal.

Krystyna was looking forward to going to school, eager for the classroom and the company of her peers. She longed to be part of a supportive, interactive community, and school seemed to offer her the first such happy engagement. Krystyna's performance on the entrance exams for a brand new girls' school named after Emilia Plater, a nineteenth-century Polish noblewoman and revolutionary, qualified her to take first-year courses. But her parents worried about the social risks. In lieu of exposing their daughter to a Polish public school, they worked to engineer a kind of internal border crossing. Benio announced to his

---

1 "For my mother and my father and my little sister."

daughter that she was to become "a citizen of the world" and attend the Lycée Français de Varsovie.

Krystyna was initially disappointed, but in hindsight she realizes that her family's decision "was the best thing that could have happened." The Lycée Français provided her with the most cosmopolitan, inclusive education that Benio's money could buy. In contrast to his thwarted efforts on Dolek's behalf, Benio was able to educate his young daughter safely in Poland for the time being, while keeping his sights on France. Warsaw's Lycée Français belonged to a global network of prestigious schools designed for the children of diplomats. Its one prerequisite was that teachers and students speak French, then Europe's diplomatic lingua franca. Thanks to her private instructors, Krystyna's French was already excellent. In addition, the Lycée required no religious instruction. Krystyna would never have to feel ostracized by sitting out a course on Catholicism that she was ineligible to take. In this way, her three adult protectors—Benio, Stefania, and Dolek—succeeded in placing her into an educational system and social milieu that removed her from the Catholic–Jewish friction pervading most Polish public institutions.

Above all, Krystyna adored attending the Lycée. This school afforded her a close-to-ideal community. While acculturated Jewishness did not alienate her from her more traditional paternal grandparents, it cut her off from the sustaining Jewish collectives to be found in one of Warsaw's Jewish public schools or Hashomer Hatzair, a Zionist-socialist youth movement that promoted scouting and sponsored summer camps and study circles. In her worldly school, Krystyna quickly grew as comfortable speaking French as she was speaking Polish. She loved studying languages, literature, and history. At the Lycée Français, Krystyna formed fast friendships with several girls, one of whom, Dagmar Pospiszel, was the daughter of a Czech diplomat. Her class's lone bully was a Soviet Russian girl with a reputation for pinching. Until the Third Reich's expansion forced her foreign friends back to their homelands and ultimately closed the school, Krystyna Bierzyńska happily studied and socialized as a bilingual "citizen of the world."

Mastering French brought Krystyna closer to her brother, the family's pioneering "global citizen." During Dolek's winter breaks and summer vacations in Warsaw in the late 1930s, Krystyna was adopted as a mascot by Dolek and his close circle of friends. She rode around on their shoulders and was squeezed into a seat of one of their big automobiles. Krystyna idolized her tall, good-looking, accomplished big brother. Dolek breathed life and youth into their Warsaw home. Krystyna recognizes now how rebellious she felt in childhood, regardless of "being a wimp" beset by illness. She first acted the rebel with Dolek, making up for years of unanswered teasing. In their last summer together before the war, for example, she balked at behaving "like a little lady" and at one point interrupted her brother's long conversation with a stranger on a train by reciting all the swear words that she had learned from her friends.

Dolek also modeled a physical toughness and spirit of adventure that Krystyna craved. He and his friends regularly went mountain climbing in the Tatras, an imposing range that forms Poland's southern border with the former Czechoslovakia. Benio approved of and envied Dolek's athletic exploits, sometimes attempting to compete with his son in sports. The more protective Stefania remained in blissful ignorance of what mountain climbing entailed. The whole family saw what Dolek was up to when he sent home a photo-postcard of himself dangling on a rope over a precipice. Krystyna remembers being impressed. Her mother, who had mainly worried that Dolek would perspire too much and catch cold on his hikes, fainted dead away at the sight.

When the opportunity arose for Krystyna to attend a summer camp near the Tatras, Dolek convinced their parents to let her go. He reckoned his too-soft little sister needed intensive toughening. The Lycée had opened the door to one accepting community. This camp, organized for acculturated Jewish children, would push Krystyna into the great world outdoors. Though it differed from the summer children's colonies that various Zionist, Bundist, and socialist organizations sponsored in that it promoted no particular ideology, Krystyna's camp echoed their emphases on familiarizing Jewish children with natural surroundings, encouraging them to become physically fit, and using athletics and sports as "a means for developing group spirit, controlled movement, and discipline."[2] These camps were organized partially in response to all the camps made available to Polish Catholic children. The ones sponsored by Jewish organizations assured both the campers and their parents of a prejudice-free atmosphere.

For two glorious summers in 1938 and 1939, Krystyna traveled south by train to the Tatras and spent a month playing outside in beautiful highland country. Each year, the camp cleverly staged small-scale Olympic games for the children, training them to compete in running, jumping, archery, discus and javelin throwing, and various team sports. Krystyna loved it all. At summer camp, her asthma disappeared, as did her usual lack of appetite. The sickly child

---

2   See, among many other publications about Muskuljudentum or "muscular Jewry," Haim Kaufman, "Jewish Sports in the Diaspora, Yishuv, and Israel: Between Nationalism and Politics," *Israel Studies* 10, n. 2 (7/2005): 151.

of the big city was transformed into a healthy, tanned girl who "was able to breathe" at last.

Krystyna's camp adventures wonderfully complemented her academic and social education as "a citizen of the world" at the Lycée. Taking part in the camp's Olympics introduced her to a larger congenial community. Her rigorous play improved her health, strength, stamina, and self-confidence. Far away from Warsaw, Krystyna fast developed into an independent young person who could navigate her way among a group of new kids. She shed her timidity and sickliness, the remnants of her cocoon, as she strived to compete and excel as an aspiring "Olympian." One incident demonstrates how much Krystyna's self-perception changed as a result. After summer camp in 1939, when she was staying with Uncle Henryk and his family in Zabierzów, Krystyna was outside goofing around with her cousin Marysia, a peer who used to intimidate her as a tough tomboy and superior athlete:

> I remember that we were sitting by a stream and throwing these little knives, Swiss army knives, into the dirt. Crazy stuff that you shouldn't let kids do. One of the knives nicked me on the leg and I started bleeding. And it was no big deal. I wasn't going to die. And I think that if that had happened at home…

"Home" in Warsaw, where loving adults hovered and overreacted, now seemed remote, irrelevant. On the very eve of World War II, the eleven-year-old Krystyna felt better able to take care of herself within the "worldly" setting of school and the not-too-rugged outdoors. She spent the rest of the summer of 1939 with her Aunt Rega and cousins Marysia and Jasiek, first in Zakopane, a famous mountain resort town, and then in Zabierzów. It did not occur to her or anyone else that her Warsaw home would suddenly turn into a dangerous place and that her anxious parents would do an abrupt about-face, pushing her to master survival skills as quickly as possible.

CHAPTER 5

Warsaw: Invasion and Occupation, 1939–1940

A great many Polish citizens savored the golden August in 1939, a summer idyll before the sweeping nightmare of the Germans' blitzkrieg. No one quite believed that there would be war, even as the German press ranted ever more vociferously about supposedly unprovoked Polish attacks on German citizens. This relative sense of well-being did not mean that Krystyna was ignorant of the dangers mounting just beyond the Polish border. Her usually protective parents did not shield her from news of Adolf Hitler and the Nazi menace. Once Germany had annexed Austria in the March 1938 Anschluss, Stefania and Benio talked at length with their Viennese friends and business partners as the latter fled through Warsaw. After Kristallnacht in November 1938, when SS troops and willing civilians mounted a massive pogrom against German Jews, Stefania spent days packing up huge boxes of clothes to send to the Jewish victims. When the Molotov-Ribbentrop Pact of nonaggression between Germany and the Soviet Union was signed on August 23, 1939, Benio made a point of explaining to Krystyna that this agreement literally wedged Poland between two mighty enemies.

Yet the German invasion of Poland on September 1, 1939, caught millions of Polish citizens by surprise. Benio and Stefania had not foreseen it. With their permission, Krystyna was whiling away the last days of her vacation in Zabierzów. The sudden war forced everyone to improvise as best they could. Despite her parents' insistence that she stay put and out of harm's way, Krystyna wrested consent from her father to come home. The German invasion very quickly destroyed her parents' power to guarantee their children safety and success. The civilized world in which a young "citizen" could flourish and circulate was crumbling on a daily basis, from one bombing raid to the next. Krystyna had to travel alone from Zabierzów to Warsaw, surrounded on the train by other tense, silent passengers, many of them in uniform.

She found 1 Piłsudski Square in chaos, transformed into a makeshift way station for army-bound and house-bound relatives. Dr. Fabian Warszawski, the dentist who had married Aunt Nina, was a captain in the reserve and had been ordered to join his unit in Warsaw. Stefania was busy gathering up the underwear and handkerchiefs that Nina had not had time to pack for him at home in Tomaszów Mazowiecki. A cousin of Stefania's named Wilek, a doctor married to a German woman, was in and out of the apartment as well, waiting on his military orders. Since the Germans had started bombing Warsaw on September 1, Benio had taken up his duties as block warden for their apartment building, looking out for air raids and helping to douse fires. He saw to it that their apartment and their section of the building's makeshift cellar were stocked with tinned goods and nonperishable staples.

Most surprising for Krystyna was Dolek's presence. Her brother had summered in southern Poland, yet, just like Krystyna, he chose joining the immediate family over personal safety—in his case, returning to a still peaceful Paris to continue his training. Dolek's decision to enlist in the Polish Army marked a major shift in his worldview. His battles with institutionalized antisemitism notwithstanding, Dolek responded to the attack on his homeland as a Polish patriot, acting as his father had when the USSR threatened a newly independent Poland's borders in 1920. The similar decisions of Dolek's close friends, who were both liberal Christians and acculturated Jews, further convinced him to take this risky step.

Dolek enlisted, however, with Bierzyński foresight, and prudently planned ways to circumvent the hazards threatening a Jewish recruit in Poland's overwhelmingly Catholic and conservative armed forces. The best strategies for avoiding antisemitic harassment involved pulling rank and hoping for educated, even sophisticated, peers—for Dolek, this meant entering the army as a doctor and an officer. The army administration was far more comfortable admitting Jews as doctors rather than "warriors," since they were accustomed to Jews working as physicians in everyday Polish society. Unfortunately, like Allied career officers elsewhere, Polish Catholic recruiters held a negatively stereotyped view of Jews' combat potential, suspecting them "of physical weakness, selfishness, cowardice, and dishonorable behavior."[1]

To ensure his acceptance and fair treatment as an officer, then, Dolek faced what could be defined as a betrayal of his family. He had to convert to Christianity. He approached this as a necessary formality, not a question of

---

1 Deborah Dash Moore, *GI Jews: How World War II Changed a Generation* (Cambridge: Harvard University Press, 2004), 27.

faith, as the one way to obtain identification papers that would protect him wherever he might be posted. Yet Dolek kept this formality secret from Benio. During the interwar period in Poland, even the most acculturated Jews usually eschewed Christian baptism. One resorted to this drastic step only for the sake of intermarriage or particular professional advancement.[2] Both Dolek and Krystyna knew that the prospect of conversion especially pained their father as a sign of disrespect to his family and a rejection of an important part of his identity. When Dolek converted to Christianity prior to joining the army in September, he secretly asked his mother to stand as witness in lieu of upsetting his father.

Once again, Dolek's example awed his little sister, though she would not be able to join the fight for several more years. Dolek sought solidarity with a Polish national collective, insofar as this was possible. He was educated and lucky enough to negotiate some of the terms of that solidarity through his medical training and conversion. Dolek had no way of knowing how horrific his military experience would be, but as it would turn out, those horrors would be due not to his Jewishness, but to Germany's allegiance with a Soviet Union eager to liquidate or absorb any potential leaders in Poland's military and civil society.

Under the terms of the Molotov-Ribbentrop Pact, the Soviet army invaded Poland on September 17, 1939, solidifying its occupation of Poland's eastern territories when the Polish army surrendered on October 6. Dolek and his unit almost immediately became prisoners of war under this Soviet occupation, a fate that his Warsaw family escaped. Dolek's service as a free Polish officer resumed only after Germany's June 1941 invasion of the Soviet Union forced the Soviets to allow for the formation of an independent Polish army under the command of General Władysław Anders (1892–1970) on Soviet soil.

On the morning of September 6, Dolek parted with his parents and sister in Warsaw. Krystyna lay asleep in her parents' bed when Dolek came in to say goodbye. Benio was off elsewhere, making arrangements. Stefania stood quietly in the room as brother and sister hugged each other. To this day, Krystyna cannot recall their farewell without crying. It meant the permanent breakup of their family. "Dolek left and the bombs fell and the next day was his birthday. He and my parents never saw each other again." For the next six years, Krystyna had to negotiate the war without her big brother's help.

---

2 Person generalizes that "baptism was seen as an act of denying one's Jewishness and almost always as a sign of opportunism" (2014, 19).

Figure 7. The Royal Palace in Warsaw in flames following German bombardment, September 17, 1939. Photographer: Unknown. In the public domain.

THE BOMBARDMENT OF WARSAW

In the meantime, the Germans' September 1939 blitzkrieg terrorized Warsaw. The Polish capital was the first European city to endure waves of heavy bombing by the Luftwaffe. The German air force leveled 10 percent of the city's buildings and seriously damaged 40 percent more, targeting hospitals, schools, and churches, as well as such historical landmarks as the Royal Castle.[3] Historians estimate that between 25,000 and 40,000 civilians were killed in the raids and accompanying ground siege. The air campaign moved very fast, beginning September 1 and culminating in massive incendiary and high explosive bombing from September 24 to 26. Jan Karski, a famed activist in and chronicler of the Polish Resistance, was appalled by the "shocking ruin" Warsaw had become after the invasion:

> The handsome buildings, the theaters, the cafés, the flowers, the cheerful, noisy, familiar Warsaw had vanished as utterly as if it had never existed.

---

3 S. J. Załoga, *Poland 1939* (Osprey Publishers, 2002).

> I passed through street after street heaped with rubble and debris. The pavements were black and grimy. The inhabitants were worn, tired, and disconsolate. Graves for the dead who could not be taken to a cemetery had been improvised everywhere in parks, public squares, and even on the streets.[4]

The Bierzyńskis quickly discovered that living in the desirable heart of the city was a great liability in war. Bombs fell on the nearby Saxon Gardens, burning up many of its huge trees and the wooden Summer Theater where Stefania and Krystyna had once attended *A Midsummer Night's Dream*. The fire spread to 1 Piłsudski Square, and the building had to be evacuated. Krystyna was too traumatized to remember her terror in the bomb cellar. But she can recall her family's nightmarish race to the Prudential Building, a big city skyscraper where the basement was reputed to be a secure shelter. As Benio, Stefania, Krystyna, and their dachshund, Żabka, headed down Mazowiecka Street towards the Prudential, they struggled against an oven-hot wind whipped up by the surrounding fires. Burning cinders whirled around them.

The fall of Warsaw on September 27 coincides in Krystyna's memory with returning to their damaged apartment. Ironically, the building itself had not been destroyed, as a falling bomb had put out the fire. Yet the interior of 1 Piłsudski Square was a shambles. The Bierzyńskis picked their way up marble stairs now littered with broken glass and rubble. In their apartment, almost all the windows had been blown out. Krystyna's aquarium had burst, scattering dead fish around her room.

Benio and Stefania adapted quickly to the new circumstances of occupation, improvising a wartime status quo. Their marriage was immediately transformed from an affluent, more or less amicable, coexistence into an intense partnership as they relied on each other's resourcefulness, pragmatism, and discipline to survive. First and foremost, they worked together to commute the Bierzyński assets into ready cash and precious stones that could be hidden easily and later redeemed. Benio turned over the reins of his business to his Christian partner, a Polonized German. He and Stefania packed up larger household valuables—silver, rugs, some furniture—and sent them to the firm's warehouse in the Praga district. The Bierzyńskis invited the warehouse watchman and his entire family to relocate in 1 Piłsudski Square, where they paid the family to carry out essential chores. The watchman and his son boarded

---
4 Jan Karski, *Story of a Secret State: My Report to the World,* foreword by Madeleine Albright (Washington, DC: Georgetown University Press, 2013), 48–49.

up what remained of the windows and biked outside of the city to buy food from local growers, while the watchman's wife cooked huge pots of cabbage and potato soup for the two families.

Krystyna recognized that the great edifice of her family's business and home was literally crumbling, yet the only household member who openly mourned the social "fall" of the Bierzyńskis was Stasia, who had left the city in September and returned later for her things. When Stefania invited Stasia to share the simple communal meal that they regularly ate with the watchman's family, their former maid sat down and sobbed. Stefania had never invested in keeping up appearances and enforcing hierarchies. Benio, a quick-witted man of action, had neither the time nor the energy to dwell on his losses during the Battle of Warsaw. In these early days of the war, Krystyna mainly remembers her parents' focus on the family's survival. As the weather turned colder in the fall of 1939 and their great showplace proved uninhabitable, the Bierzyńskis abandoned 1 Piłsudski Square and moved in with Aniela and Adolf in their more modest Polna Street apartment, which had escaped bombing damage. They were lucky to be alive and together with their extended family.

THE NAZI CAMPAIGN AGAINST THE JEWS

Once the German authorities began ostracizing Jewish Varsovians, Benio and Stefania had to confront just what they had moved to Warsaw to escape. In cosmopolitan interwar Warsaw, a Jew with means could be almost anybody, as Benio and Dolek had struggled hard to prove. Jews could be secular, modern, debonair, worldly, athletic, and patriotic. A Jew could speak fluent Polish or fluent French and exist as a citizen of the world. Even acculturated Jewish Varsovians could be proud of being Jews, for their Jewishness was one attribute of their complex urban identity and they lived in a city where Jews made up a third of the population. During the occupation, the restrictions, humiliations, and punishments that the Nazis enforced on Jewish Varsovians negated these positive traits and diverse possibilities by declaring all Jews to be uniformly undesirable. Nazi policy and practice aimed to isolate and then liquidate all Jews as subhuman vermin.

Krystyna most vividly recalls the different ways her father resisted the initial stages of the Nazis' Final Solution in Warsaw. On the one hand, Nazi persecution evoked his fierce sympathy for the Jewish Varsovians who first suffered its cruelty. After years of not enlightening his daughter about the preponderance of Orthodox, Yiddish-speaking Jews in the capital (an estimated 84 percent of the Jewish population there),[5] Benio suddenly felt compelled to teach Krystyna empathy and respect for them. During the first weeks of the Nazi occupation, father and daughter were walking together near their apartment when a big open truck filled with Orthodox Jews screeched to a halt in front of them. Armed German soldiers threw the men onto the ground. The soldiers yanked the prisoners by their beards, beat them until they were bloody, and then prodded them to clear the rubble in the street. Krystyna had never seen such violence in her life and desperately wanted to look away. But Benio demanded that his daughter bear witness. "You have to look at this and never forget it," he told her. It was important to him that she see the atrocities committed against the Jews and be outraged by their suffering. For the first time in Krystyna's life, Benio willed his daughter to feel solidarity for those many different Jews whom she had never known.

On the other hand, Benio refused to identify himself and his family members with other Jews in the city in compliance with Nazi orders. When the new Governor General Hans Frank decreed on October 23, 1939, that all Jews were required to wear the yellow star, the Bierzyński family did not obey. "We will never wear the star," Benio told his daughter. Warsaw Jews were deeply divided on this point; some singled out those acculturated Jews who refused to wear the star as unprincipled and even cowardly, accusing them of renouncing their inconvenient heritage.[6] Benio's decision seemed more calculated to defy the occupiers than to deny his background. In his estimation, the Nazis had created the yellow star and the white armband to make their dirty work easier. His gutsy refusal meant that he, Stefania, and Krystyna did not endure the separateness and stigma that these symbols inflicted—the sudden painful alienation that writer Jerzy Jurandot describes in his memoir on living in the Warsaw Ghetto:

> I had such a strange sensation when I saw people without armbands on the street. Up until now they had been my colleagues, acquaintances, fellow patrons at cafes and movie houses. My own people. And suddenly—because I wore that white rag around my right arm—a wall rose up between us. An invisible wall, but no less real than the one that separated

---

5 Antony Polonsky, "Warsaw," *The Yivo Encyclopedia of Jews in Eastern Europe*, accessed June 9, 2017, http://www.yivoencyclopedia.org/article.aspx/Warsaw. Polonsky cites that the Jewish community was 83.7 percent Yiddish-speaking and Orthodox in the 1897 census.

6 Person also points out that "many assimilated Jews nonetheless chose not to comply" (2014, 27).

the Ghetto from other districts. These were no longer my people, but a world closed to me. They were Aryans.[7]

Like other acculturated Jews who could pass physically as Aryans, Benio chose to defy death at the Nazis' hands by ignoring their edicts. He and his wife and daughter never wore the yellow star or the white armband. Nor did they join the huge procession of Jews whom the Germans ordered to move into the newly walled Ghetto in the fall of 1940. Such resistance was by no means easy. It meant living in constant terror and, very often, debilitating loneliness. Any Jew apprehended as trying to pass as an Aryan was automatically sentenced to death. Many Jewish Varsovians moved into the Ghetto, as Jurandot did, to stay close to their family members and friends and in the vain hope that they would be less harassed by thieving, abusive Germans once they consented to live in their own separate space.[8] For example, Krystyna's Aunt Aniela and Uncle Adolf moved to the Ghetto once the Bierzyńskis left Warsaw altogether in 1940. When they still lived on Polna Street, they had been robbed and Adolf beaten by a marauding German soldier. Aunt Nina also ended up in the Ghetto because she could not bear to live apart from her daughter and son-in-law.

While Benio's first response to Nazi persecution was powered by his outrage and nerve, he could not maintain that resistance on his own for long. He and Stefania received essential support from their Christian friends in the capital. For example, they took counsel with their trusted neighbor, Amelia (née Raczkowska) Brzozowska, the photographer's wife. A highly intelligent, attractive, well-connected woman, Amelia was a devout Catholic. Yet her advice to the Bierzyńskis stemmed from her wish to help, not proselytize. She worked in the front office of her husband's studio and managed to learn a great deal from the many Germans who lined up there to be photographed. Amelia's clientele boasted to her that their superiors were planning major punitive actions against Warsaw's Jews. Alarmed, she urged Benio and Stefania to protect themselves and Krystyna with baptismal certificates, their surest means of protection. Stefania and Dolek had protected Benio from news of Dolek's conversion months before, but Amelia's news of dramatically worsening conditions convinced Benio himself that their conversion—at least as attested on paper—was essential.

---

7 Jerzy Jurandot, *Miasto skazanych. Dwa lata w Warszawskim getcie,* ed. Agnieszka Arnold (Warsaw: Muzeum Historii Żydów Polskich, 2014), 55. Translation mine.
8 "Fear of repression is cited in many diaries as the principal motivating factor [in moving to the Ghetto], but there was also undoubtedly an element of safety offered by enclosure within the ghetto walls" (Person, 2014, 29).

The Bierzyńskis' family baptism was carried out as a strictly contractual affair. Before the war, Benio had been a generous contributor to a variety of charities, including a Catholic church that had awarded him a certificate in gratitude for his large donation. Amelia presented this certificate as proof of the family's worthy candidacy for conversion to Catholicism in the Church of the Holy Cross, a congregation housed in an impressive baroque structure located opposite the entrance to the University of Warsaw, several blocks east of the Bierzyńskis' apartment building. Benio, Stefania, and Krystyna consequently received their baptismal certificates in this famous church, which served as the resting place for the remains of the composer Frederic Chopin and the Nobel Prize-winning writer Władysław Reymont. Most importantly, the devout Amelia stood as godmother to Krystyna, and she undertook her role as spiritual mentor and surrogate parent very seriously. The religious commitment of a good Catholic woman to the young Jewish charge whom she loved proved to be an invaluable lifeline later in the war.

A TASTE OF CONSPIRACY

Even as her parents were figuring out strategies for survival in occupied Warsaw, they managed to place Krystyna in another wonderful school before they quit the capital. In early 1940, the Bierzyńskis and the Zylbers moved together into a "very modern" apartment in Ochota, a district southwest of the city center. As a result, Krystyna was enrolled in the Wanda Szachtmajerowa (Shakht-may-er-OV-a) High School in Ochota, a prestigious girls' school founded and built in the interwar period. During those decades, Wanda Szachtmajerowa guaranteed its students a rigorous and progressive education, requiring them to learn about their cultural and natural environment and engaging them in what today would be called "service learning" or social/philanthropic work. The school attracted the offspring of the elite (including Piłsudski's two daughters, Wanda and Jadwiga), and awarded scholarships to less-privileged girls. It practiced religious tolerance by employing teachers of different faiths to give religious instruction to their specific communities. The Wanda Szachtmajerowa uniform, consisting of a white blouse with a sailor collar, a green skirt, and a dark green beret with a black pompom, was well-known throughout the city, and was a uniform that Krystyna could wear with pride.

The Nazis, however, were adamant about denying education to the occupied. As they moved from a program of persecution to extermination of Polish

Jews, they ultimately forbade Jewish children any kind of schooling in 1942. In the case of Polish Christians, whom the Nazis deemed subhuman, fit only for slave labor, all post–grammar school education was forbidden by the spring of 1940. Universities were shut down, and existing secondary schools were either transformed into vocational training centers or closed.

In issuing such edicts, the Germans underestimated Polish citizens' longstanding expertise in withstanding foreign occupation and repression. During the 123 years of the Partitions (1795–1918), when Poland had been divided up and occupied by three different empires—Russia, Prussia, and Austria-Hungary—Varsovians, who lived in the Russian partition, developed many ways to preserve Polish culture, language, and national memory through unofficial networks and clandestine practices. It is no wonder that the Polish Resistance movement during World War II became the most extensive and best-organized in Europe. A single interwar generation of Polish citizens separated one set of conspirators from another. As Stefan Korboński, the last chief of the Resistance, explains, the prospect of resuming this activity during the occupation excited him:

> I was still young enough to feel the attraction of an armed struggle, with its sporting Chances, its surprises, and its Great Adventure written in capitals. My own generation, which grew up during the twenty years of Poland's independence, envied its elders their conspiratorial past, which was enveloped in an atmosphere of mystery and heroism. Conspiracy never ceased during the century-long struggle for independence, and with the restoration of that independence it occupied a place of honour in the hearts of the Polish people.[9]

Krystyna's admission to Wanda Szachtmajerowa High School could not have happened at a more opportune time in her life. The school offered her acceptance, purpose, and her first taste of resistance. Attending Wanda Szachtmajerowa initiated Krystyna, a Jew hiding in plain sight, into the thrilling subterfuge of Polish political conspiracy. The administrators at Wanda Szachtmajerowa High School succeeded in keeping their doors open by promising the German authorities that they would only teach their female students how to sew. The teachers, in turn, continued to offer their students

---

9 Stefan Korboński, *Fighting Warsaw: The Story of the Polish Underground State, 1939–1945*, trans. F. B. Czarnomski (Funk & Wagnalls, 1965), 11.

the usual high-school level courses. They also drilled the girls in stowing away their textbooks and hauling out their sewing as quickly as possible if a German inspector paid a visit. For the record, Krystyna did learn how to darn socks at Wanda Szachtmajerowa. But she mainly studied her academic subjects and was swept up in the school-wide drama of outfoxing the occupiers. She would resume this heady conspiratorial work when she returned to her country of Warsaw in 1942.

CHAPTER 6

Learning the Life of a Fugitive, 1940–1942

During a recent trip to Poland, I visited what is called "the old cemetery" in the town of Zabierzów. After an hour of treading carefully along the narrow, weed-slippery lanes between packed graves, I finally found the granite headstone that Krystyna erected for her father in 2014. Zabierzów's old cemetery served only the Christian community, but this restriction posed no problem for Benio. His Christian first name of Bronisław is paired with the already polonized Bierzyński, and his birth and death dates are marked by the customary Christian star and cross. Bronisław Bierzyński's headstone commemorates the symbolic and actual resting places of two other Bierzyńskis—his wife, Stefania, who died either in a Warsaw prison or the Treblinka death camp, and his sister-in-law Regina (Rega), Henryk's wife, whose body was recovered from a hilltop where the Germans had executed her and other Jews as part of a roundup. Rega's family was able to identify her remains after the war because her murderers had overlooked the wedding ring on her finger.

Figure 8. Headstone for the graves of Bronisław (Beniamin) Bierzyński, Stefania Bierzyńska, and Regina Bierzyńska in the old Zabierzów Cemetery. Photo by author.

The descending list of names on this headstone conveys the rapid erosion of Krystyna's support system in her early teens, the death of one parent after another during the first three years of the war. In 1939, Benio had already begun suffering from chronic constipation and other intestinal problems, the first symptoms of the colon cancer that would metastasize to his liver.

Krystyna, Benio, and Stefania had moved south to Zabierzów as her father's cancer spread. Henryk arranged for a renowned Kraków surgeon to operate on his brother in May 1940, but the procedure was not a success. As Benio grew weaker, Stefania had to take charge. Zabierzów provided her with the closest approximation of a retreat and a hospice. The small town afforded her a quiet, relatively safe place to nurse Benio, immediate access to her brother-in-law's medical help, and the company of Henryk's family to normalize life for Krystyna. Stefania rented the lower story of a small house owned by a railroad worker named Faryna. The modest lodgings that Benio, Stefania, and Krystyna occupied consisted of a kitchen, a bathroom, and a larger room where everyone slept. The Farynas, their landlords, lived upstairs. An outhouse stood in the back yard that expanded into open fields. It was in this house that Benio died on January 28, 1941, surrounded by his family, with his pain eased by the morphine his brother administered to him. For the next two days, Benio Bierzyński's body was laid out in the kitchen, illuminated by candles and awaiting burial in Zabierzów's Christian cemetery.

Benio's decline and death from natural causes happened terribly fast for his daughter. His death also marked the passing of his Warsaw dream of a cosmopolitan, opportunity-filled life for himself and his family in Poland's greatest metropolis. The Nazis' occupation and relentless persecution of the Jews in Warsaw forced him to die in small-town exile.

STEFANIA THE CONSPIRATOR

It was during this exile that Stefania supervised every aspect of Krystyna's welfare. With her characteristically even-tempered competence, she taught her daughter a great many things by word and example. Stefania's attitude and abilities normalized her daughter's descent from a cushioned life of affluence in the big city into a fugitive's constantly improvised existence in provincial Poland. In Zabierzów, Stefania took over the roles that she would have delegated to servants in Warsaw—housekeeping, nursing, even cooking. Krystyna recalls the delicious stew that her mother concocted out of horse meat, though no mention was made of the secret ingredient until dinner was over.

Even as Stefania tended to Benio, she saw to her daughter's education with whatever resources she could muster. She first made do with local teachers, allowing Krystyna to take lessons from her cousin Marysia's tutor in town. Stefania also hired Wiktor Jassem, a brilliant student of languages, to teach Krystyna English, a skill she hoped would serve her daughter well after the war. Jassem grew up to become a world-renowned specialist in phonetics, teaching in Kraków's prestigious Jagiellonian University. Krystyna thought that the young Wiktor was fresh and "repulsive," and insisted that her mother keep the kitchen door open during their lessons in the main room.

When these piecemeal tutoring arrangements proved unsatisfactory, Stefania implemented a new plan utilizing her contacts with the Polish Underground. She located a good instructor willing to break Nazi prohibitions on secondary education and teach Krystyna history and mathematics in his Kraków apartment. This meant that Stefania had to coach her daughter on how to pass as an Aryan. Every week Krystyna had to manage the train trip from Zabierzów to Kraków and back on her own. It is telling that Krystyna remembers neither her teacher's name nor his address, but can retrace how she made her way to his home. Stefania calmly mapped her daughter's route from train station to streetcar stop to apartment building. She devised a regular detour for Krystyna's return home, protecting her from a long risky wait at the train station where German soldiers tended to loiter and might have pestered her with too many questions. After every lesson with her tutor, Krystyna stopped at one of Kraków's few open cafeterias (what the Poles call "milk bars") to order some tea and a watery bowl of soup as a means of killing time and steadying her nerves. Krystyna acquitted herself very well under her mother's tutelage, managing to "pass" with the requisite confidence, "extraordinary discipline, and self-control"—no easy feat for a twelve-year-old.[1] The only attention the blonde-haired, blue-eyed girl attracted from the German soldiers were compliments about her looks.

In effect, Stefania was training her daughter in conspiratorial skills, the purposeful action and unruffled behavior that would enable her to live under constant German surveillance. How this retiring, bookish woman mastered these strategies herself remains a mystery. Stefania's sensitivity to others and seemingly serene character enabled her to operate very well under cover.

---

1 Gunnar S. Paulsson, *The Secret City: The Hidden Jews of Warsaw, 1940–1945* (New Haven, CT: Yale University Press, 2002), 108.

Krystyna's memories of her mother during this time echo Karski's observations about Polish women's success in the Resistance:

> My own experience has led me to believe that women on the whole make better conspiratorial workers than men … . They are quicker to perceive danger and less inclined to avoid thinking about misfortunes than men. They are indubitably superior at being inconspicuous and generally display much caution, discretion, and common sense. The average woman who takes up secret political work evinces much more "Underground common sense" than the average man. Men are often prone to exaggeration and bluff, an unwillingness to face reality, and, in most cases, are subconsciously inclined to surround themselves with an air of mystery that sooner or later proves fatal.[2]

Stefania herself intuited how to handle far more difficult and dangerous missions than passing as an Aryan, and took phenomenal risks on her family's behalf. Once Benio had been moved to Zabierzów, Stefania traveled alone to the Nazi-built ghetto in the city of Częstochowa, a three-hour train ride from Zabierzów, and freed her interned mother-in-law by bribing the right German official. Krystyna wonders at her mother's chutzpah: "Money we had, and she knew how to do it! Nobody taught her. She *knew*." Stefania restored Berta, still formidable in her early eighties, to her two sons and their families in Zabierzów. She came to rely on the older woman's strength and family devotion, and Berta and Stefania grew very close as they nursed Benio together.

After Benio's death, Stefania constantly assessed and juggled family needs. Krystyna's welfare was paramount, yet her child seemed to be in no grave danger in the spring of 1941. Stefania thought she could rely on her in-laws in Zabierzów to care for her daughter whenever she was needed elsewhere. Krystyna spent most of her time with her young cousins in town. Stefania also felt reassured about Dolek's fate after she received the postcard he was able to send from the USSR through the Red Cross. She could not know how miserable and endangered Dolek was in a Soviet prison camp. But Stefania was painfully aware of how terribly her sisters and their families were suffering from overcrowding, food shortages, and increasing violence in the Warsaw Ghetto. She managed to keep in regular contact with Aniela, Adolf, Nina, and Nina's grown children through Underground ties and, remarkably enough, calls via the phone lines to the Ghetto that the Germans never bothered to cut.

---

2 Karski, 2013, 262.

Figure 9. From left: Marysia Bierzyńska (Krystyna's cousin, Henryk and Rega's daughter), Krystyna, and unknown man. Zabierzów. Taken between 1940 and 1942. From collection of Krystyna Bierzyńska Stamper.

Stefania therefore decided to help those loved ones whom she knew to be in the greatest peril. She started making trips to Warsaw, hauling food, medicine, and probably cash to her sisters in the Ghetto. She could not sit in Zabierzów and let her family die. Stefania exemplified the sort of secret Jewish hero who has been maligned rather than recognized in Holocaust history, as historian Gunnar Paulssen argues in his paradigm-shifting study of the "secret city of Jews"— approximately 28,000 in Warsaw—who were kept alive through the efforts of 70,000 to 90,000 anonymous helpers. Paulssen points out that past analysts would have labeled someone like Stefania an "evasionist," a convert or acculturated Jew "who never entered the Ghetto, or left it at an early stage," and consequently was "anathematized by most Jews" as a traitor. Instead, Stefania was both brave and discreet, as Paulssen explains: "in truth, [such Jews] often brought assistance to relatives and friends within the Ghetto, and later found hiding places for them and helped to smuggle them out." In lieu of the simplistic notion of Jewish victims saved by Gentile rescuers, Stefania incarnated a form of "Jewish self-help."[3]

---

3 Paulssen, 2002, 5, 27.

Indeed, Stefania succeeded in saving a blood relative from the Warsaw Ghetto in summer 1941. By this time, a typhus epidemic was raging in the Ghetto—an epidemic emphatically not the product of the horrible Nazi caricatures of "unclean Jewish vermin," but brought about by the Germans themselves through the Ghetto's deliberate overcrowding and the authorities' refusal to fix burst water pipes in winter, which resulted in sewage piled high in the streets. As Jurandot attests in his memoir, one did not "walk" in the Ghetto, but squeezed oneself through tightly packed crowds of people to get from point A to point B.[4] Stefania risked her life to nurse her infected brother-in-law Adolf. He died in her arms. She then bribed German guards so that she could smuggle her widowed sister Aniela out of the Ghetto and back to Zabierzów. Aniela never recovered from Adolf's death, but she served as best she could as an adult guardian for Krystyna during Stefania's several trips to Warsaw.

THE GERMAN ROUNDUP IN ZABIERZÓW

Even after Adolf's death and Aniela's removal to Zabierzów, Stefania's work in the Ghetto was far from over. Her youngest sister, Nina, was there, doing her best to support her pregnant daughter, Wanda, and Wanda's husband. Krystyna recalls Wanda before the war as a vivacious young woman, a student at the University of Warsaw who specialized in English language and literature. Wanda sometimes dropped by for dinner at the Bierzyńskis, delighting Krystyna with her emancipated views and demonstrations of the latest dances. Now Wanda's situation in the Ghetto was desperate, her life and her unborn child's life dependent on her aunt's help.

At this time, Stefania faced family crises on two fronts. By the summer of 1941, the Germans had expanded their campaign of rounding up and executing Jews throughout Poland, including the countryside around Kraków. News of an imminent local raid caught all the family members in Zabierzów by surprise. Stefania was away, tending to her sister's family in the Ghetto. Somehow Stefania orchestrated Krystyna and Aniela's rescue long distance, enlisting the help of her landlord Faryna to move them out of harm's way.

Stefania's specific rescue efforts were well-conceived, though the Germans never bothered to search Faryna's place. Faryna did as he was instructed, taking Krystyna to the presumed safe space of a little farm nearby. Aniela urged her niece to go by herself. It was not clear to Krystyna if her aunt thought herself

---

4 Jurandot also describes the German genesis of the typhus outbreak (2014, 105–11).

Figure 10. Krystyna's Aunt Nina and her family: from left, Wanda Warszawska (daughter), Dr. Fabian Warszawski, and Dr. Janina (Nina) Warszawska. From collection of Krystyna Bierzyńska Stamper.

a burden or was simply ready to die. Other members of the Bierzyński family, however, were caught in the roundup and killed. What Krystyna can recall of her terrifying flight may have become conflated with what she subsequently heard about the murders of her grandmother Berta and Aunt Rega:

> Aniela said, "Go, child, go." But Aniela stayed. My dog stayed, too. No questions were asked. It was dawn. We went through the kitchen and out the little back porch, past the outhouse and into the fields. We climbed up a hill and you could see the main road if you were way up there. I'm sure I cried or something. I had no idea where I was going.
>
> And we went up that little incline and I looked down at the road. There were horse-drawn carts carrying Jews on the road, carts filled with all their pillows and bedding, pots and pans. Now I am probably imagining it, but I think I saw my grandmother. I think I saw my aunt. This may be a figment of my imagination. I don't remember Germans, but there were probably guards. But I think I saw my grandmother and my aunt in one of those carts because, yes, they were taken away like this.

> I was alone with Faryna. I had no idea where I was going. We climbed up and away from the road to this little farm with a dog and a horse and a cow and a young couple. It is very cloudy in my memory. I was very afraid. I was completely alone. I had no idea who these people were. I didn't know what they were going to do to me. I didn't know how long I was going to be there. I didn't know who was going to come get me.

Whether or not Krystyna witnessed her relatives being carted to their place of execution, the images of their violent deaths, seen or later superimposed, remain embedded in her memory. In the fall of 1939, Benio had forced Krystyna to watch the Germans beating Orthodox Jews in the middle of Warsaw, a horrible sight of unfamiliar people suffering. Now the Nazi terror hit close to home, killing beloved relatives whom she saw almost every day. In the small town of Zabierzów, Krystyna "watched" with a stranger as the Germans dragged off her beautiful Aunt Rega and infirm Grandmother Berta. They caught Rega very soon after she had sent her two children to hide in the woods. Berta, whom Krystyna had come to admire and love, had been hauled out of her son Henryk's apartment on a stretcher by the Germans for the sole purpose of killing her in a public roundup of Jews. The soldiers had found Berta alone in the house because she had broken a hip trying to change a light bulb by herself. When news came of the raid, Berta had insisted on staying behind, refusing to endanger the rest of the family with her immobility. While Krystyna had survived this roundup, she had done so alone and at a high psychological cost. What she has retained of this traumatic experience are feelings of paralyzing fear and helplessness and a vision (real or reconstructed) of her loved ones borne off to their deaths.

After the Germans' raid on Zabierzów's Jews in 1941, Stefania was able to create one last, rather primitive refuge for her daughter and sister. The three moved to the village of Podłęże (Pod-WEH-zhe), located east of Kraków on the railway line, where they shared a room. Stefania had acquired new papers that identified her as Stefania Zakrzewska, and she passed herself off to her new landlords, a young farmer and his older wife, as a widowed seamstress. Krystyna would learn soon enough about the importance of devising a plausible story of one's new identity and possessing the false papers to prove it. The room that Stefania had rented had a clay floor and shared a wall with the kitchen, where the farmer's wife baked bread every day. That oven kept the three tenants warm through the winter of 1941–1942.

The clay floor had its uses as well. Stefania and Aniela dug up the soft section nearest the oven and there buried a jar full of gold coins, a custom-made Schauffhausen watch, and a bracelet studded with large and small diamonds. The women tamped down the clay and placed a bench over the spot to make it less conspicuous. The diamond bracelet, Benio's gift to Stefania when Krystyna was born, was worth roughly $25,000 American dollars when he purchased it in 1928. The precious stones embedded in each link of the bracelet would see Krystyna through the rest of the war.

For roughly another year, until summer 1942, Krystyna's life was governed mainly by the rhythm of rural Catholic Poland, which was soothing in its predictability. The landlords accepted Stefania, Aniela, and Krystyna as Polish Catholics and never pressed them for information. Krystyna liked the couple, particularly the simple and affable wife, and she worked with the two farmers in the fields. The physical exercise invigorated her. In Zabierzów, she had grown accustomed to roaming the fields with her cousin Marysia, and she missed spending time outdoors. Stefania and Krystyna also joined the wife in going to mass, making excuses for Aniela's absence since her aunt's dark coloring and perpetual depression might have raised questions. Such precautions may not have been necessary. When Krystyna took lessons with the nuns at the local church, she guessed that they knew that she was Jewish and they were hiding Jewish children as well.

During this period, Krystyna came to embrace the Catholic church as an oasis of comfort and strength. She knew that churchgoing constituted camouflage, reinforcing their landlords' and neighbors' perception of their Christian identity. Yet Krystyna mainly kept going to mass because, as she acknowledges, she liked it: "It has always filled a very emotional need for me. I don't agree with a lot of the stuff that the Catholic Church preaches, but I love my place in it. I feel very comfortable, very nurtured." When Benio had decided that his immediate family would be baptized for safety's sake, he surely did not anticipate his daughter's need for spiritual consolation and community. Benio had accepted and honored his father's piety as a Jew; one wonders if he would have felt the same way about his daughter's newfound piety as a Catholic.

What upset Krystyna in Podłęże were her mother's trips to Warsaw. Stefania did not spell out her reasons for going, perhaps because she did not want her decisions questioned or the dangers envisioned. The same unimaginable horrors that compelled Stefania to help family imprisoned in the Ghetto would only torment a child already fretting about her mother's absence. Yet

Krystyna could not know that her mother's silence was meant to protect her. She simply felt abandoned. When her mother would return from her Warsaw trips, exhausted and sore, Krystyna did not hold her fire: "Why must you do this? Why don't you just stay here?" These unanswered questions continue to torment Krystyna, more than seventy years later.

Why Stefania Bierzyńska, alias Stefania Zakrzewska, chose to make another trip to Warsaw as the Ghetto was being liquidated in summer 1942 remains unclear. German troops were rounding up Ghetto residents by the thousands and marching them to the *Umschlagplatz*, where the Jews were forced into cattle cars bound for the Treblinka death camp. No one was spared, not even the orphanages that the German authorities and the *Judenrat*, or Jewish Council, had promised to save. It would have been insanely risky for Stefania to attempt any rescue missions. From what Krystyna has been able to reconstruct, however, Stefania was not caught in the Nazi *Aktion* in the Ghetto, but instead picked up on one of Warsaw's main streets on the Aryan side, a Catholic Varsovian ostensibly going about her business. Someone, maybe a disgruntled former employee of Benio's, fingered Stefania as a Jew and reported her to a Polish policeman. Stefania was hauled off to Gęsia Prison or Gęsiówka, a concentration camp within the city. She was either executed there or sent to Treblinka and killed in its gas chambers.

Caught in such dire straits, Stefania, the self-taught conspirator, kept her wits about her. Before she disappeared, she arranged to get word of her situation to a trusted friend in the city, someone who could be depended on to alert Krystyna and Aniela. Soon after Stefania's imprisonment at Gęsiówka, a Polish policeman called on Dr. Nina Marczewska. The policeman slipped Marczewska Stefania's wedding ring, a note about her whereabouts, and instructions for her daughter and sister's welfare. He also gave her the talisman that Stefania always carried with her—the letter from Dolek delivered to her from the USSR through the Red Cross.

Krystyna never received her mother's ring. Doctor Marczewska wisely urged the policeman to keep it as payment for services rendered. The doctor also immediately sent Stefania's message to Podłęże: It was imperative that Krystyna and Aniela leave their hiding place and return to the capital, where the Bierzyńskis had devoted friends. Though Stefania was forever lost to her daughter, her last undercover act secured Krystyna's safety once more. That she was able to do so was a matter of incredible luck and a testament to her nerve, devotion, and a network of Gentile friends and anonymous helpers in the Resistance.

Learning the Life of a Fugitive, 1940–1942 • CHAPTER 6 | 47

KRYSTYNA'S FLIGHT TO WARSAW

Stefania's disappearance and message mobilized Krystyna to return to her dangerous hometown. She was not merely following her mother's orders, but determined to find her mother. She could not believe that Stefania had vanished without a trace. It was an extraordinary solo mission for a fourteen-year-old girl to undertake. Aniela had no intention of traveling with Krystyna, at least in part because she considered her "look" a liability for her fair-haired niece. Krystyna's resolve and self-possession demonstrated just how thoroughly she had absorbed her mother's training and example. Like her mother, she would make the journey alone.

With Aniela's help, Krystyna girded herself for the trip with Bierzyński valuables. Aniela sewed the diamonds from the bracelet into the waistband of one of her niece's skirts. Krystyna also carried a few $20 gold coins in a little bag and packed her mother's flowered silk spring dress, which she clung to as memento and talisman, together with a few other clothes in a suitcase. She left wearing a winter coat and kerchief because the weather had already turned cold, but that did not prevent her from shaking while armed German soldiers paced back and forth at the Podłęże station. Krystyna remembers this first lonely departure as "the most frightening moment of her life."

Unfortunately, her initial attempt to reach Warsaw, "booked" through Underground connections who assessed where she would be safest at any given time, took her roundabout from Kraków to Tarnów to the big eastern city of Lwów. It was a very difficult dry run for what would prove to be an easy final trip. Krystyna handled herself remarkably well, despite her fear and setbacks. Peasants carrying a basket of chicks scratched her leg as they walked through her third class car to Tarnów; by the time she reached Lwów, the scratch was clearly infected. Krystyna sought out a doctor in the city on her own. Though the doctor recognized how dangerous the infection had become and treated it properly, he warned her never to come back. As Krystyna later discovered, Lwów in the fall of 1942 was a very dangerous place for Jews on the run.

Krystyna's short detour to Lwów exposed her to the crazy contradictions of war. During her train ride to the city, German officers who noticed her sitting alone became concerned about the welfare of a pretty young blonde girl traveling "without her mother." For safety's sake they moved her to their car up front, where they fed her bread and sausage. These strange benefactors did not pry into her circumstances. In striking contrast, Krystyna's supposed safe house in Lwów itself turned out to be doubly dangerous. There the lone adult in charge, a drunkard, began to beat his teenage daughter during the night, prompting the neighbors to call the police. Terrified by the man's violence and her own potential discovery, Krystyna violated her instructions the next morning, telegraphing her aunt in code to see if the coast was clear in Podłęże. No one had disturbed Aniela. Krystyna returned to the still hospitable farm from her first attempt to reach Warsaw with a patched-up leg and a head full of lice. The farmer's wife was happy to see her again, incurious about where and why she had gone away.

Krystyna's second attempt to reach the capital was successful, with the exception of a near stand-off in Kraków. She had been told to obtain her identity papers through her mother's distant cousin, the Polish Jewish doctor named Wilek whom she had first met in her Warsaw home at the very beginning of the war. When Krystyna knocked on his door, however, Wilek's German wife opened it and sized her up as trouble. Before Wilek's wife could push Krystyna out, the girl stuck her foot in the door—an act of self-assertion by a now rather seasoned fugitive. After Krystyna insisted on getting her fake identity papers, or *Kennkarte,* the German woman grudgingly made arrangements, and then threw this dangerous fourteen-year-old out of her house. A few hours later, Krystyna received the papers from a shady-looking stranger as she waited in an outdoor café. It was as if she were playacting in an espionage film, even though she was far too young for the part. Nevertheless, Krystyna boarded the train to Warsaw with no further mishap. She was determined to visit her mother's last contact—Doctor Nina Marczewska. It was October 1942.

CHAPTER 7

Warsaw: A Conspiratorial Identity, 1942–1944

Krystyna reached Doctor Marczewska's Warsaw apartment just before the Germans' wintertime curfew of 7 p.m. She knew the way by heart. In Kraków that morning, Krystyna had been thrown out on the street as soon as she had wrested help from a hostile German. But in Warsaw that same evening, Doctor Marczewska pulled Krystyna inside as soon as she opened the door. The symbolism could not have been clearer. Krystyna had found a home once more in Warsaw, though her family and circumstances had completely changed.

That home was extremely dangerous, however, particularly for Krystyna's welcoming host. Doctor Marczewska was not merely sheltering a young Jew, but also was under surveillance because her husband, the Minister of Agriculture during the interwar period, had been arrested by the Germans and was being held hostage in the dreaded Pawiak Prison. Doctor Marczewska did not hesitate to bring Krystyna into the fold, putting her up for the night and contacting other people whom the Bierzyński family knew and trusted so that they could work together on the girl's behalf. Despite her situation, Marczewska accepted the great responsibility that a desperate Stefania had laid at her door. She saw to Krystyna's welfare and continued to console the girl as she repeated what she knew of Stefania's disappearance and certain death.

KRYSTYNA'S NEW FAMILY COUNCIL

Soon after Krystyna's arrival, three smart, resolute women met somewhere in Warsaw, joining forces to mastermind their de facto ward's survival in the city. On Krystyna's recommendations, Doctor Marczewska summoned Amelia Brzozowska, the elegant, resourceful family friend who had pledged to be Krystyna's godmother at her baptism, and Zofia Raczkowska, Amelia's sister-in-law and the wife of a doctor who was a good friend of the Zylbers. Zofia's husband, Doctor Raczkowski, had enlisted in 1939. His family did not yet realize that he, along with tens of thousands of Polish army officers, had been executed by the Soviet secret police in Katyń. Though Zofia Raczkowska knew Krystyna the least, her contributions to the girl's well-being were key. She provided Krystyna with two homes—one the safe place where the girl could be registered and attract little notice, the other her own apartment where Krystyna found the greatest emotional refuge.

First and foremost, the trio needed to fabricate Krystyna's new identity—a new name, biography, pretext for local residence, and well-forged identity papers, the *Kennkarte* that the Germans constantly demanded for inspection. It turned out that the papers Krystyna had bought for twenty dollars in Kraków were so ridiculously flawed that they would have condemned her to a concentration camp. The false surname on the Kraków papers was Łabędź, that of a well-known Jewish veterinarian. Amelia and Zofia enlisted the aid of Andrzej Barucki, a male relative deeply involved in the Resistance, to put together a better fake identity.

Krystyna's new papers bore the unremarkable name of Zofia Łabędzka, a girl whose residence was remote from 1 Piłsudski Square. Zofia Łabędzka would be registered in an apartment on the corner of Wawelska and Uniwersytecka Streets in Ochota, the southwestern district to which Krystyna and her parents had retreated before leaving Warsaw. The apartment belonged to Irena Cudnowa, Zofia Raczkowska's widowed sister. According to the new story, Zofia Łabędzka, who had been born and raised in the western Polish town of Sosnowiec, had been forced out of her home by incoming German settlers. Her parents had found lodgings elsewhere, while Zofia's "Aunt Irena" offered her niece sanctuary in the capital. The arrangement behind the legend was mutually beneficial. Whereas Krystyna required a reason and a relative for her sudden move to Warsaw, Irena, now retired, was in search of paying boarders. The two rehearsed their cover story for several days and could repeat it to Barucki's satisfaction when he delivered Krystyna's papers.

Krystyna's new identity required a makeover as well, according to the fashion-conscious Amelia Brzozowska. Regardless of her supposed roots in provincial Sosnowiec, Krystyna was groomed as a chic, adolescent Varsovienne, a mature-looking fourteen-year-old. Amelia insisted that Krystyna wear lipstick, have her hair cut stylishly, dispense with wearing kerchiefs (the mark of a country bumpkin), and be outfitted with several pretty new dresses. Her guardian reasoned that a well-dressed, nicely coiffured city girl was less likely to be perceived by the Germans as a Jewish orphan on the run.

Warsaw: A Conspiratorial Identity, 1942–1944 • CHAPTER 7

With two years' practice behaving as an Aryan in smaller towns and inter-city trains, Krystyna quickly adjusted her behavior to Warsaw standards. She was eager to circulate in the big city, the hometown she had never been free to explore. The youngest in her biological and now surrogate family, Krystyna was not burdened by survivor guilt or housebound by terror of the outside world. Other young Jewish women who "passed" in big cities such as Lwów and Warsaw had to overcome major psychological hurdles before they could venture out in public. In her memoir about surviving "under false identity" in wartime Poland, Blanca Rosenberg remembers that she spent several weeks hiding in her hosts' apartment. She did not know how to project normalcy after her child and beloved brother had been killed by the Nazis and she herself had escaped the horrific Kolomyja Ghetto:

> For two weeks I stayed inside, too frightened to leave the house. My host and hostess reassured me that I looked my part perfectly, and no one would suspect me. With my blond hair braided into a crown, I was assured that I looked like a German Fräulein or a Slavic peasant girl. I had to break out and begin moving around the town establishing a normal way of life. All I had to fear, they said, was the fear haunting my eyes and the sadness of my demeanor. "You look like you've just come from a family funeral." Exactly! I didn't know it then, but it was that fear and the funereal air that continued to give me away in the years that followed.[1]

Due to wartime food shortages and the rationing of such utilities as gas and electricity, Krystyna's home life was not as pretty and bright as the stylish persona she assumed in public. When the authorities switched off electricity at night, she and her landlady Irena relied on smoky oil lamps and carbide lights. Like many other Varsovians, Irena bought herself a small wood-burning stove for cooking and warmth. Its heat filled the kitchen, but not the bedrooms down the hall. Irena and Krystyna warmed their ice-cold beds with glass bottles filled with heated water, an inadequate, uncomfortable substitute for rubber hot water bottles. Bathing became a chore since all the water had to be heated in the kitchen. Krystyna soon got into the habit of having her hair shampooed at a beauty salon.

Living as the paying boarder of a retired middle-aged woman liberated Krystyna from the normal domestic chores of a middle-class daughter (or

---

1 Blanca Rosenberg, *To Tell At Last: Survival Under False Identity, 1941–1945* (Urbana: University of Illinois Press, 1995), 82.

dependent niece), though she appreciated Irena's work as housekeeper and cook. She remembers, for example, the filling kasha soup or *pensak* that Irena cleverly prepared, boiling buckwheat overnight and covering the secured pot with blankets during the day so that they had a hot, cooked meal by evening. Irena's bed doubled as an improvised slow cooker. Krystyna, in turn, was a reliable boarder. Every so often, she would remove another diamond from her skirt banding and redeem it for cash at a jeweler's on Marszałkowska Street, a gentleman whom her guardians recommended for his honesty and discretion.

No one could replace Krystyna's parents when she returned to "her country" of Warsaw. It was tremendously difficult for her to accept the fact of her mother's death, which contrasted starkly with her father's passing. In Zabierzów, Krystyna had witnessed the merciless progress of Benio's disease, his slipping away in body and consciousness. She had sat through her father's "Catholic" wake and attended his burial in a snowy Christian cemetery. But Stefania had disappeared into thin air, leaving behind her letter from Dolek and instructions for the care of her daughter and sister. Krystyna had no way to fill in this blank. Her new family network insisted that she avoid those Warsaw sites where Stefania had taken care of family and perhaps lost her life—the Ghetto where roughly 60,000 out of 400,000 had eluded deportation, and the city's prison and concentration camp. Krystyna was not allowed to search for other relatives in the Ghetto, though she suspects now that her cousin Wanda and her husband fought and died in the April 1943 Warsaw Ghetto Uprising. These places were deathtraps for any Pole, let alone a Jewish teenager openly searching for her family. For the most part, Krystyna obeyed her guardians. Just once she attempted to visit her old apartment building, hoping that lipstick and a new haircut would suffice as disguise, but her nerve failed her when she spied the familiar cobbler in their courtyard.

Krystyna found solace in the warm family atmosphere of Zofia Raczkowska's apartment on St. Barbara's Street. This beautiful place was enormous, like Krystyna's former home on Piłsudski Square, occupying an entire floor of its building. Here, she felt loved and cared for by her surrogate family, especially by two young people whose age made them seem like older, wiser siblings and whose temperament gently verged on the parental. One was Zofia's daughter, Basia, seven years older than Krystyna and a nurse in training, who lived there along with their kindly housekeeper, Helenka. Zofia also took in boarders, and luckily attracted a widowed engineer and his adopted son from Białystok to rent her drawing room. The son, Stefan Zacieniuk, became the second surrogate sibling for Krystyna, a gifted painter and possibly an orphan of an affluent, even aristocratic, Russian family. The stars aligned for the sensitive, charming Basia and Stefan, whom Krystyna describes as "a beautiful man": "Basia played the piano, and Stefan and Basia sort of got together—to begin with, there was just attraction, and then there was romance, and then I arrived on the scene. And I became their sister."

Krystyna's sibling relationship with Basia and Stefan was profoundly therapeutic. She talked openly with them about her family and painful past. Excellent listeners, they surrounded her with love, respect, empathy, and devotion. Krystyna vividly recalls how Basia, alerted by a phone call from home, raced back from a lecture to give her "sister" a shot of Asmalin during a

Figure 11. Wartime photo of Basia Raczkowska. From collection of Krystyna Bierzyńska Stamper.

Figure 12. Wartime photo of Stefan Zacieniuk. From collection of Krystyna Bierzyńska Stamper.

bad asthma attack. The experience of the attack and Basia's immediate response broke down Krystyna's defenses, allowing her to grieve openly, to cry for her mother even as Basia held her in her arms. With Basia and Stefan, Krystyna did not have to hide her sorrow or worry that they would abandon her. Their protectiveness, somewhat reminiscent of her parents' cocooning, was more comforting than constricting: "They hovered over me. And they were everything to me. They were my social connection. They were everything." In Basia and Stefan, Krystyna found a "family" equipped to understand and soothe a deeply wounded, rebellious teenager.

KRYSTYNA THE CONSPIRATOR

After the cataclysmic losses she had suffered over the past three years, losses that had required her family to retreat into southern small-town Poland, Krystyna was spoiling for action in her big city hometown. At Doctor Marczewska's apartment that first night in Warsaw, Krystyna was thunderstruck when Marysia, the doctor's seventeen-year-old daughter, calmly asked her if she smoked.

Figure 13. Dr. Janina Marczewska and her daughter in later years. Seated bottom left: Dr. Janina Marczewska. Standing from left to right: Grażyna Stęcka (Krystyna's cousin, granddaughter of Matylda Bierzyńska Stęcka): Monika Marczewska, and Dr. Marysia Marczewska (daughter of Janina Marczewska). From collection of Krystyna Bierzyńska Stamper.

A successful solo mission through enemy territory might count as a major accomplishment, but being able to smoke—that struck Krystyna as the height of adult chic. It turned out that there was a silver lining to being on her own in Warsaw. She could try out adult behaviors she had never before been allowed. Cooped up with Irena every night after curfew, Krystyna found release and pleasurable diversion in the apartment across the landing, where the good-looking Tadzio Genneło lived, the son of a well-known Warsaw architect. She had attracted her very first boyfriend.

Krysytna's new home harbored bolder scofflaws. Irena's two other boarders operated an illegal business on the premises. A couple whom Krystyna "just knew were Jewish" had removed the gas meter, bribed the meter man to keep quiet, and cooked molasses into moonshine, or *bimber,* overnight in Irena's kitchen. They paid Krystyna to watch their homemade still while she did her homework, and she also earned extra cash distributing bottles of *bimber* to bars. No one reported the couple to the authorities, which seemed surreal to their student employee because "the smell of the molasses cooking was so strong."

Krystyna did go back to school soon after she moved in with Irena, and eventually returned to Wanda Szachtmajerowa High School once her guardians realized that no one would confuse the more mature Zofia Łabędzka with a Krystyna Bierzyńska who had studied there two years before. As Krystyna recalled this era in her life, however, she did not dwell on the excitement of clandestine education. She was far more eager to talk with me about the politically illicit connections she made at work. By 1942, obtaining work and the accompanying work card was imperative for Polish teenagers, for this proved that they were training to be laborers and not studying illegally toward positions above their "racial capacity." A work card could save a teenager from being detained, interned, or shot during a raid.

Doctor Marczewska arranged for Krystyna's employment in a store that fixed and sold electric cords and plugs to Poles and the occasional German. The work was unchallenging and the pay supplied her with pin money, but the main attraction was her coworker, Alla Wysocka, an older girl involved in the Resistance. Alla introduced Krystyna to a Warsaw of restless young people who frequented coffeehouses serving ersatz coffee (the only kind available) and sometimes ham sandwiches, a luxury most Varsovians could only dream about. Krystyna felt so guilty about devouring these sandwiches that she could not confess the fact to her new family. Some of the young people whom Krystyna encountered made money on the black market, like the couple cooking moonshine at Irena's place. Others were engaged in resisting the occupation, contributing to and distributing underground publications, plotting small and big acts of sabotage, and talking a great deal about a major action in the city. Alla's boyfriend would end up playing a role in assassinating Franz Kutschera, the head of the Warsaw Gestapo, on February 1, 1944. He would later die, as did hundreds of other Varsovians, as the Nazis carried out fierce retaliatory raids.

Krystyna was thrilled to be admitted into the outer circles of political conspiracy, circles dominated by young men and women who were at once deadly serious about their work and intoxicated by their own daring. At one meeting organized by the Polish Scouts, Krystyna laid eyes on her first underground newspaper, titled *Antena* (Antenna). She would later serve as a courier for such publications. By the end of 1942, after two months in the city, Krystyna had resolved to break one of the cardinal rules of the Nazi occupation: spending the night in a place where she was not officially registered. Krystyna was intent on seeing in the new year of 1943 with her conspiratorial crowd. She threw caution to the winds, informed Irena of her plans, and left her poor landlady to fret about the consequences all night.

Krystyna cannot recall if the party took place in the Warsaw district of Powiśle or Żoliborz. Alla was her guide, and they ended up in an apartment packed with boisterous, excited young people. She soon found out that Germans were living in the apartments located directly above and below them. Warsaw's occupiers also loved celebrating *Sylwester*, the name commonly given New Year's Eve parties throughout Central Europe because the Feast of Saint Sylwester, a fourth-century pope, falls on December 31. When the Germans knocked on their door at midnight, the Varsovian kids were not sure what to expect. Fortunately, their neighbors, already well into their celebration, only wanted to contribute some bottles of champagne to the young people's party. It was at this party, lubricated by German champagne, that Krystyna first heard talk about an uprising, "that something big was going on that I wanted to be part of."

Emotionally anchored by Basia and Stefan, swept up in the company of other young conspirators, Krystyna felt how much easier it was to not be seen as a Jew in occupied Warsaw than in the southern Polish countryside. She understood that the people she socialized with on the Aryan side, the only place her new family permitted her to be, were not interested in talking about who was or was not a Jew. Krystyna was very lucky. At school, at work, in the coffeehouses, or at meetings, her peers seemed to abide by a "don't ask, don't tell" policy. This likely stemmed from the fact that explicit identification was deadly to both Jews *and* the Christians who "failed" to denounce Jewish friends and acquaintances to the Germans. For example, Krystyna was quite sure her boyfriend Tadzio from across the landing realized that she was Jewish, but, as she reminded me, "you just didn't talk about that."

In the one instance where a past acquaintance, also Jewish, was imprudent enough to flag her down on the street, Krystyna immediately recoiled. Tekla Frankiel, a girl she knew from prewar summer camp, alarmed her as loud and oblivious. When Tekla showed her the little room she was renting and invited her to move in, Krystyna realized just how dangerous it would be for two Jewish girls to live together on their own. She appreciated how wisely her new family had plotted her new identity, placing her with a plausible relative and reinforcing the lessons her mother first taught her about blending in and behaving with confidence and discretion. Krystyna simply did not trust Tekla as a responsible actor, in both senses of the word.

THE WARSAW GHETTO UPRISING

The ability to pass, be it as an "Aryan" or a nonconspirator, became especially urgent by spring 1943. In January of that year, the Jewish Combat Organization and the Jewish Military Union, composed mainly of young people hiding in the Ghetto, thwarted the first German attempt at a final deportation of Jews through a self-sacrificing attack on SS and police units marching people to the Umschlagplatz. When the Ghetto resistance leaders obtained information that the Germans planned another such attempt on the eve of Passover, April 19, 1943, they launched the Warsaw Ghetto Uprising, shooting at entering German troops from their makeshift bunkers. As Marek Edelman, the last surviving commander of the Uprising, explained to writer Hanna Krall, it did not matter if the insurgents were effective snipers: "The important thing was just that we were shooting. We had to show it. Not to the Germans. They knew better than us how to shoot. We had to show it to this other, the non-German world. People have always thought that shooting is the highest form of heroism. So we were shooting."[2] Over the next twenty-seven days, until May 16, the poorly equipped Ghetto defenders held out against strengthened German forces with vastly superior weaponry. Krall totes up the stark imbalance:

> For instance: there were 220 insurgents, 2090 Germans.
> The Germans have their air force, artillery, armored vehicles, flamethrowers, 82 machine guns, 135 submachine guns, 1358 rifles. Each insurgent, according to the report of the uprising commander's deputy, has one pistol,

---

2 Hanna Krall, *The Subtenant: To Outwit God,* trans. Joanna Stasinska Weschler and Lawrence Weschler (Evanston, IL: Northwestern University Press, 1992), 133.

five grenades, and five incendiary bottles. There are three rifles in each area. For the entire Ghetto, there are only two mines and one submachine gun.[3]

The Ghetto fighters' defeat was imminent once SS General Jürgen Stroop, the commander in charge of repressing the Uprising, ordered that Ghetto buildings be burned to the ground and systematically bombed. As the fires drove survivors into the basements of the buildings, the Germans used sound-detection devices to track down and kill those who were still alive.[4] Of the estimated thirteen thousand Jews killed during the Ghetto Uprising, almost half perished in the fires, either burned alive or asphyxiated by smoke. Stroop celebrated the defeat of the Uprising with one last monumental act of fiery devastation, blowing up the Great Synagogue on Tłomackie Street.

Figure 14. German destruction of housing block at the intersection of Zamenhof and Wołyńska Streets in the Warsaw Ghetto during the Ghetto Uprising. Photographer unknown. In the public domain.

Not yet fifteen years old, Krystyna read about the progress of the Warsaw Ghetto Uprising in the underground press. All too soon, the fires set by the Germans literally shrouded entire districts of the capital with the evidence of

---

3 Ibid., 218.
4 Ibid., 222.

Jews resisting and dying in its flames. Though her home was located almost five miles away from the Ghetto, Krystyna could smell the smoke and see the fire, especially at night:

> When you think about where the Ghetto was and where Ochota was, I guess the wind was blowing that way. The sky was red. There was flame and smoke. It was horrible. You knew that people were burning. We [Irena and Krystyna] opened the windows [on the Uniwersytecka Street side of the apartment]. It was April, as you know, and there was a red arc before us. Irena had her arm around me. I knew I probably had relatives burning there, but there was nothing we could do. Nothing.

The devastation of the Warsaw Ghetto terrified and tormented Krystyna. The Ghetto had killed her Uncle Adolf with typhus and, very likely, her Aunt Nina and cousin Wanda by fire. The extreme deprivations her relatives had suffered in the Ghetto had led Krystyna's mother to her death. Krystyna's new family sternly warned her to steer clear of the Ghetto, curtailing her visits to Doctor Marczewska's clinic and home on Długa Street, which stood right opposite a Ghetto wall. Krystyna learned only after the war that Doctor Marczewska and her daughter Marysia had been deported to Ravensbrück, a large women's concentration camp in Germany, sometime before the 1944 Warsaw Uprising. They told her of their wartime ordeal during her first return trip to Poland in 1967.

In the meantime, Krystyna came into contact with Jews who had escaped the Ghetto's inferno and were scrambling to hide or pass as Aryan outside its walls. For a while, a little Jewish boy regularly visited the Raczkowska apartment in the middle of the night to get food. Their housekeeper Helenka always had something prepared for him. Then he stopped coming. Krystyna recalls riding on a tram where she instantly spotted several Ghetto refugees—"frightened people on the streetcar, going somewhere." Their bewildered, terrified look made her acutely aware of controlling her own expression. It was a matter of survival to dissociate from those who projected what Blanca Rosenberg so aptly described as "the fear and funeral air" that kept giving her away. As Jewish cabaret artist Stefania Grodzieńska remembered from her own escape from the Ghetto to the Aryan side, local knowledge, nerve, and some acting skill could mean the difference between life and death. Grodzieńska praises her mentor,

Fryderyk Járosy, a famous cabaret director in hiding, for training recently escaped Jews how to pass:

> During 1942–1943, as the Ghetto was being liquidated step by step, Járosy's room became a way station through which scores of illegal refugees passed. There they received the first tips: the cost of a tram ticket or a loaf of bread, how to comb your hair, which expression will give you the best "look." This phenomenal director and creator of stage characters never guessed that his art would one day save human lives .... [His students] left his place changed, with the belief that they would survive, which of course did not guarantee that that would always be the case.[5]

Krystyna's most positive encounter with a Jew her age affirmed her Jewishness in a way she was not yet equipped to appreciate. Months before the Warsaw Ghetto Uprising, she made the acquaintance of a young man ostensibly named Olek, whom she knew to be Jewish. Olek was tall, dark, and very good-looking. He and Krystyna met in the coffeehouses and went on walks, exchanging carefully edited stories about their past. Olek was a fabulous pianist, but an evening concert after work—even for one person—was out the question because of the early winter curfew. So Olek made do by performing for Krystyna over the phone, stunning her with his rendition of George Gershwin's *Rhapsody in Blue*. This performance was a magnificent gift for Olek to share with a girl he liked. It also might have been a dangerous provocation if Olek was living in a place where his neighbors were unhappy or suspicious about an impromptu piano piece played loudly next door. In any event, Krystyna never heard from Olek after this extraordinary phone concert. She guessed that he had been picked up by the Germans.

To this day, Krystyna adores *Rhapsody in Blue* and is moved by the memory of first hearing it played by a young Jewish man in occupied Warsaw. The significance of this shared music, however, goes beyond Olek's ability and Krystyna's awe. We will never know why Olek decided to play Gershwin's famous piece. But his choice reflected the preference of major popular composers in interwar Poland, almost all of whom were acculturated Jews. Composers such as Henryk Wars, Jerzy Petersburski, Henryk Gold, Artur Gold, and others created distinctive variations on the ragtime, swing dance, and jazz music

---

5 Stefania Grodzieńska, *Urodził go Niebieski Ptak* (Warsaw: Wydawnictwa Radia i Telewizji, 1988), 37. Translation mine.

pouring out of the United States from the first decades of the century—music by African American composers that immediately inspired songs, dances, orchestra pieces, and even operas by Jewish American composers. The Nazis had outlawed all such music as degenerate. Many urban Polish citizens embraced this music regardless of Nazi restrictions, but would have identified Gershwin's work as American rather than Jewish, just as they would have characterized the songs and dances of Petersburski and other Jewish composers as Polish rather than Jewish. And yet Jewish artists were truly the creators of Polish swing and jazz. In effect, before he disappeared, Olek entrusted a girl he liked with Jewish treasure, a classic of modern music written by one of the greatest Jewish and American composers of all time.[6]

EVERYDAY TERROR IN WARSAW

Apart from the great horror of the Ghetto's destruction, viewed from afar, Krystyna witnessed and narrowly escaped everyday acts of German terror against Varsovians. In one instance, Krystyna was a room's length away from a German roundup and public execution. She was having her hair shampooed at her regular salon near the major Warsaw intersection of Aleje Jerozolimskie and Marszałkowska Street when trucks suddenly braked in front of the shop. The salon staff quickly closed the drapes and hustled their clientele into a little room at the back. The Germans shoved their prisoners onto the sidewalk, shot them dead, threw their bodies back into the trucks, and drove away. Krystyna later heard that there were Jews among those murdered. Such sudden public executions were designed to demonstrate the enormous reach and speed of German "justice": to impress on Varsovians, often in well-traveled public spaces, that "Jewish vermin" and "Polish bandits" (the Nazi slurs that were expediently assigned to whichever random victims they seized) would be hunted and killed relentlessly. Such roundups aimed to snuff out compassion and incipient rebellion in the local populace with a lethal spray of machine-gun fire.

Krystyna likewise witnessed how these deadly demonstrations backfired into an endless symbolic struggle. The Germans' attempt to terrorize failed quite spectacularly. At night, Varsovians would wash away the blood and human

---

6 Beth Holmgren, "Cabaret Nation: The Jewish Foundations of the Polish-Language Literary Cabaret." Forthcoming in *Polin: Studies in Polish Jewry*, volume 31 (estimated date of publication: 2018).

remains left on the sidewalk and, in their place, heap flowers and candles to honor and rehumanize the victims. Every evening, German troops would clear away these tributes, only to find them restored by sunrise. It was clear that the resisters were willing to risk their lives to show the solidarity and resistance that the Germans presumed they could scare away.

The Germans' intensification of terror and the Varsovians' dogged resistance took an all-too-real toll on human lives. Yet this symbolic battle also supercharged the act of living, especially for young people determined to strike back. Leokadia Rowińska, four years older than Krystyna and deeply involved in the planning of the 1944 Uprising, summarizes the heightened danger and drama of this period:

> Yes, life did go on. Amid the ruins and sidewalk graves—some of them still there since 1939—and the bullet-ridden walls of executions with flowers and lighted candles deposited in front of them (illegal demonstrations according to the authorities), life, in fact, had blossomed. People did live, love, and die every day as if nothing else mattered. They actually lived and loved even more intensely, simply because it was so easy to die. They were dying by the hundreds in almost daily public executions, or would disappear without a trace during the roundups that overcrowded prisons and camps.[7]

The "don't ask, don't tell" policy of not speaking about one's Jewish identity continued in the Resistance after the Warsaw Ghetto Uprising—at least in Krystyna's experience. The reports about the Ghetto's ordeal that she read in underground publications represented Jewish fighters with admiration and sympathy. Yet the Resistance in which Krystyna took an ever more active part presumed that all its members were Catholic Poles. In the absence of her biological family, this posed no crisis of conscience in Krystyna. Unlike her parents, she had embraced the conversion to Catholicism as a matter of faith and a means to spiritual strength and community. When the Church's holidays and rituals were overtly politicized by the Resistance, Krystyna felt doubly drawn to participate. She particularly remembers joining the wartime public processions on Good Friday. On this most somber Christian holy day, Catholic Varsovians walked from one church's symbolically decorated grave to another, praying and reflecting on the crucifixion of their Lord. In occupied Warsaw, the gravestones bore incendiary messages such as "freedom" and "Fatherland" or the symbol

---

7 Leokadia Rowińska, *That the Nightingale Returns: Memories of the Polish Resistance, the Warsaw Uprising, and German P.O.W. Camps* (Jefferson, NC: McFarland, 1999), 68.

for "fighting Poland" (*Polska walcząca*), the letter "P" anchored below by a "W." A slow stroll from grave to grave with a cohort of one's peers could easily provoke a German roundup. After all, these young people were paying tribute to a religious exhibit at least partly designed by and for "bandits." Krystyna recalls spending several hours visiting graves in the city center, moved by the sight of them even as she worried about what might happen to her and her friends.

One other particularly Polish event remains vivid in Krystyna's memory, in an interesting juxtaposition to the "concert" that Olek played for her over the phone. The Germans outlawed not only "degenerate Jewish music," but also the national compositions of the conquered. In defiance of this ban, the Polish Resistance organized secret concerts of Polish classical music for those who had been vetted for their loyalty. Krystyna attended one such event—a piano recital of Frederic Chopin's work. The organizers planned well to keep both concert and audience from being detected. They covered the windows of a second-floor apartment somewhere on Mokotowska Street with curtains and mattresses for secrecy and soundproofing. Attendees slowly filled the room. Krystyna was thrilled by the music and felt a proud, intimate sense of belonging: "Outside our boys were clearly guarding the entire block, so that in case anything happened, we could disperse. Nothing happened. And we listened to music and it was wonderful. Unforgettable. That was part of being a patriot: we listened to Chopin."

Linking herself with the young people in the Resistance, committing herself to that "something big" in the future, Krystyna achieved the transcendent state of solidarity in wartime Warsaw that she had been longing for her entire childhood. It was a longing that her father likely had hoped to fulfill in moving to Warsaw and following Piłsudski, the impulse that compelled her brother, a young man all too familiar with institutionalized Polish antisemitism, to join the Polish Army and distinguish himself as a doctor on the battlefield treating Polish troops. Ever since her semester in 1940 spent camouflaging serious study with sock darning at Wanda Szachtmajerowa High School, Krystyna had been attracted to this noble version of Polish national resistance. Upon her return to Warsaw, she had the great good fortune of being cared for by a surrogate Polish family who were united in loving and worrying about her. Moreover, the new young friends whom Krystyna made through work and semiconspiratorial socializing accepted her without questioning or objecting to her Jewishness. Krystyna felt no tension even when her identity seemed known. She interpreted the blanket silence about Jewishness as a protective tactic devised for wartime conditions.

At the same time, Krystyna's perception of what constituted Polish patriotism was mainstream and, on most points, enthusiastic. She had not been raised to know any alternative, save being "a citizen of the world," a stance rendered impossible by the war. Krystyna's knowledge of her Jewish identity consisted almost entirely of her love for and pride in those members of her family whom she knew and liked best, an identity that mixed together different and sometimes contradictory goals and traits: the drive to be educated and cultured, love of reading, a penchant for the "good stuff," extroversion, introversion, impulsiveness, discretion, ministry to others, and a passion for grand adventure through physical and financial risk.

Krystyna's Jewish identity had not been shaped by any form of Judaism or Jewish religious practice; a sense of a Jewish political and messianic destiny through Zionism or socialism; or education about the many and diverse Jewish cultural achievements in Poland and the European diaspora. Therefore, when Olek presented Krystyna with Gershwin's *Rhapsody in Blue*, she loved it as a magnificent piece of music and Olek's personal gift to her. She heard Gershwin out of context. Yet when the Resistance organized a clandestine group concert of Chopin's marvelous compositions, Krystyna knew to value this music as both "wonderful" and "patriotic." The Polishness conveyed by the Resistance was ethnically uniform and entwined with Catholicism. Krystyna's Jewishness remained a private family affair.

After the Warsaw Ghetto Uprising in spring of 1943, Krystyna's involvement with the Polish Resistance grew more intense and hands-on. Though she as yet had not taken an oath to serve the Home Army, the fighting force that would carry out the 1944 Warsaw Uprising, she began training in first aid with the eventual aim of becoming an orderly. Her training sessions consisted of several people meeting with a nurse in a hospital room at a specified time, so as not to attract general attention. In the course of five lessons at a hospital near Warsaw's Old Town, Krystyna learned very basic first aid: how to clean and dress a wound; where and how to apply a tourniquet; and how to distinguish peroxide from iodine and use both correctly.

Krystyna's summer of 1944 began with a jolt and then subsided into lazy, hot weeks of living in the moment. On June 6, 1944, she was traveling through the center of the city, hanging onto a strap in the streetcar along with dozens of other Varsovians as the Germans sat comfortably in the front seats reserved for them. As usual, the streetcar piped in German popular music to boost the morale of the occupiers, jolly German drinking songs such as Albert Graf Schlippenbach's "Ein Heller und ein Batzen" (1830) that the soldiers loved. Suddenly the music was interrupted by a local radio broadcast. A Polish speaker announced that the Allies had landed in Normandy, France, and the first notes of the Polish national anthem resounded before the transmission was cut off. The streetcar erupted:

> Everyone went crazy. They were hugging and crying and screaming. The Germans just cowered. Then everything went quiet. Nobody got arrested, nobody got shot. The Germans just sat there. And then the German music came back. That was the beginning of the end.

The interruption of German music on public transport was unprecedented—an impressive flexing of the Resistance's young muscles. It was by no means as serious a threat to the Germans as was the assassination of Kutschera, the Warsaw Gestapo chief, four months earlier. Nevertheless, the fact that this D-Day announcement was broadcast and provoked no repercussions reinforced the general perception among Varsovians that the Germans were on the defensive. Krystyna told me that she and her friends already knew about trains carrying horribly wounded German soldiers back from the Soviet front. The Red Army was pushing its way west, liberating territories from German occupation.

Yet the early summer of 1944 afforded Krystyna a wonderful oasis from the war, reprising, to a different extent, her happy summer camp experiences in 1938 and 1939. Before the war, Krystyna's summers spent near the Tatras had toughened her up, improving her health and bolstering her confidence. By 1944, after five years of loss, danger, and hardship, Krystyna did not require toughening, but the indulgences of normal adolescence. She needed to sleep, eat, and goof off. She had just turned sixteen in May, and her body craved the sort of rest and nourishment that wartime conditions had denied.

It is important to reiterate here that Krystyna's surrogate family formed a group of intimates quite separate from her friends in the Resistance. Doctor Marczewska and her daughter had disappeared, but the Raczkowskis, Amelia Brzozowska, and Stefan Zacieniuk provided her with sanctuary, care, and love until Krystyna was marched out of Warsaw with other insurgents in October 1944. As it happened, these branches of her family shared a summer place bearing the glorified name of "villa" in the little town of Świder, just twenty minutes by electric train from Warsaw. The town took its name from the river Świder, a tributary to the Vistula, and it was known as an unpretentious, delightful summer destination for Varsovians.

Figure 15. Krystyna and Basia Raczkowska in Świder in the summer of 1944. From collection of Krystyna Bierzyńska Stamper.

Figure 16. Krystyna relaxing in Świder in the summer of 1944. From collection of Krystyna Bierzyńska Stamper.

During the very hot months of June and July 1944, Irena, Basia, Krystyna, and Stefan traveled to Świder to relax in their plain cabin with its old furnishings and front deck and to swim, walk, and sunbathe by the river. Basia, Krystyna, and Irena frequently stayed overnight, the two young women talking about everything and nothing and giggling when Irena scolded them about going to bed. Stefan visited during the day and sometimes Zofia and even Amelia made the trip to take a swim. For the time that they were outside of Warsaw, they unplugged themselves from the war, soaked in the local natural beauty, and stuffed themselves:

> We gathered blueberries and bought strawberries. It was wonderful. We ate strawberries with sour cream. Somebody made strawberry soup. We'd be sitting outside with big soup spoons, and, of course, there were flies everywhere. While I scooped my spoon into the soup, two flies fell in. I just picked them out and kept eating.

Świder lingers in Krystyna's memories as a stay in paradise. Safe and carefree, indulged and sated, her sixteen-year-old self luxuriated in the pleasures of a normal adolescent summer vacation. Zofia Łabędzka, the new identity she had donned upon coming back to Warsaw, at last took a little holiday, letting the real Krystyna relax with family members who knew all her secrets. Krystyna is convinced that these replenishing days and nights in Świder enabled her to survive the rest of the war.

CHAPTER 8

The 1944 Warsaw Uprising

The positive impressions Krystyna formed about the 1943 Warsaw Ghetto Uprising were filtered through that "non-German" world where, as Marek Edelman claimed, shooting represented the highest form of heroism. *The Information Bulletin*, the Home Army's main press organ, announced the Poles' change of heart about the Jews after the latter had transformed themselves, in Polish estimation, from victims into fighters. The *Bulletin* reported that, while the Poles had been horrified by "the display of Jewish passivity in the face of slaughter" during the Great Liquidation of summer 1942, they marveled at the action, bravery, and unfazed resistance of Jewish fighters during the April 1943 Uprising. Furthermore, Poles were moved when the fighters erected a Polish flag alongside a flag featuring the Star of David over the Ghetto, thereby making common cause with the Polish Republic in battling their German oppressors.[1]

While many Varsovians on the Aryan side tried to compartmentalize the horrific torching of the Ghetto as the Nazis' peculiar campaign against the Jews—to say nothing of those residents who were satisfied that the occupiers had "solved" their Jewish question—the Ghetto Uprising, the first major act of armed resistance in the wartime capital, fundamentally affected all those in the Resistance waiting impatiently for their turn to fight. These future soldiers and volunteers could observe the power of a slightly threatened German war machine in action: their utter disregard for the humanity of their enemy as they annihilated men, women, and children; their systematic torching and bombing of all the Ghetto's buildings; and their dogged apprehension of fugitives in building basements and the city sewers. Witnessing the Ghetto Uprising and its merciless repression first- or second-hand accustomed more Varsovians to perceive the entire city as a battleground and resolved them to work as a

---

1 Quoted in Joshua B. Zimmerman, *The Polish Underground and the Jews, 1939–1945* (Cambridge: Cambridge University Press, 2015), 374.

gigantic defensive collective if they were to resist the Germans effectively. Yes, Varsovians had endured a highly destructive invasion in 1939. But the razing of the Ghetto now exposed them to the possibility of an apocalyptic finale.

THE PUSH FOR AN UPRISING IN WARSAW

For the military leaders of the Home Army and the thousands of young people ready to serve, the mission of the Warsaw Uprising seemed at once a national imperative and a plausible success. The generals of the Home Army, with Tadeusz Bor-Komorowski at the fore (1895–1966), were planning the Uprising in close consultation with the Polish government in London exile, reacting to a political and military situation very much in flux. They believed that the Germans would retreat quickly from Warsaw, as the Reich was being pummeled by Allied forces in the west and the Soviet Army in the east. They also presumed that the Nazi leadership had been shaken to the core by the attempt to assassinate Hitler on July 20, 1944.

These exiled politicians and in-country generals also feared that the Soviet Army would free Warsaw on its own and install their hand-picked Polish Committee of National Liberation (PKWN) as the capital's new leaders. As historian Joshua B. Zimmerman cogently argues, their fears were grounded in fresh precedents. When Home Army units successfully liberated the eastern Polish cities of Wilno and Lwów together with the Soviet Army, the First Polish Army under the command of General Zygmunt Berling (a Polish branch of the Soviet forces) "was brought in to replace the Home Army, whose officers were being summarily arrested … . And once the Soviets crossed the Bug [River] into formally recognized Polish territory, the Polish Committee of National Liberation declared itself the de facto government of liberated Poland."[2]

The Polish leaders, therefore, were counting on a brief lull in the fighting during August 1944 as the Germans withdrew forces from the city and the Soviet Army was only on the verge of entering it. At this point, they would deploy the largest number of soldiers in the Home Army on the "immense and dramatic stage" of Warsaw to lay claim to the capital for the Second Polish Republic. They would muster a show of popular support and strength that would impress Churchill and Roosevelt and warn off a poaching Stalin.[3] A successful Uprising

---

2 *Ibid.*, 383.
3 Jan M. Ciechanowski, *The Warsaw Uprising of 1944* (Cambridge: Cambridge University Press, 1974), 272

might at last convince the Western Allies to stop appeasing the Soviet Union, which had broken off diplomatic ties with Poland's government-in-exile, located in London, due to the Polish insistence on a formal investigation of the mass graves of Polish officers massacred on Soviet soil at an earlier point in the war.

Logistically and historically, Warsaw was the best place to make a stand for independent Polish sovereignty. Exploring the various reasons "why Warsaw rose," historian Jan M.Ciechanowski points to the Varsovians' repeated readiness and valor in revolting against the Russian empire: in 1794, when Tadeusz Kościuszko mounted his insurrection; in the uprisings against the authorities in the Russian partition in 1830 and 1863–1864; and during the revolutionary years of 1904–1907. Over the course of the Nazi occupation, the Resistance and the Home Army naturally concentrated in and spread out from Warsaw, "which meant that only in Warsaw could the course of the battle and the process of emerging into the open be personally directed and controlled by the leaders of the underground state."[4] Warsaw would function as a symbol of all Poland when the Uprising was launched.

Outside of Poland, experienced commanders such as Kazimierz Sosnkowski and Władysław Anders harshly criticized the in-country generals' decision to unleash the Uprising as "a hopeless gesture of self-immolation."[5] They recognized that the highly disciplined German Army was reinforcing its Warsaw units in anticipation of an advancing Soviet Army; in consequence, the Soviet Army was encountering fierce military resistance as they fought their way to the Polish capital. Generals Sosnkowski and Anders, both far from occupied Warsaw, could not know how desperately the rank and file of the Home Army wanted to liberate Warsaw themselves. The Uprising, so long in the works, promised the Home Army its absolute moment of cathartic glory. General Bor-Komorowski possessed neither the temperament nor the discipline to convince his troops to stand down, as Ciechanowski concludes:

> During five years of painstaking and dangerous preparation there had developed a sense of anticipation so intense, and so diffused through all sections of the Home Army and the population at large that, at the climax, a decision not to rise would have been more difficult to make, and would have required more mastery of self and the situation, than the decision which Bor-Komorowski finally made on 31 July 1944.[6]

---

4 Ibid., 274.
5 Zimmerman, 2015, 382; Ciechanowski, 1974, 262.
6 Ciechanowski, 1974, 276.

Krystyna vouches for the fact that the young people in the Home Army were primed for the Uprising to be launched and were optimistic about its outcome. She remembers her amazement when, during the final days of July 1944, German soldiers ceded her the sidewalk, as if acknowledging that Poles no longer needed to defer to the occupiers. On August 1, as Home Army soldiers and volunteers purposefully walked to their stations, the Germans seemed to melt away. On this "hottest day of the year," young men donned trench coats to hide the machine guns they were carrying. As Leokadia Rowińska observes, Varsovians citywide seemed aware of what was to come and ready to play their part:

> The city looked as if all its inhabitants had decided to take their vacation at the same time and were on their way to their chosen vacation spots. Practically everyone was carrying a large suitcase and many were dragging huge packages, which obviously contained heavy equipment.... [Those carrying skis] were medics bringing stretchers to their designated medical stations.[7]

THE UPRISING BEGINS

Once the Uprising erupted on August 1, 1944, it turned the city inside out. Those who had trained (more or less) for different duties assumed their roles as soldiers, medics, orderlies, and couriers. Civilian residents helped the Home Army prepare the city for battle, building barricades in the streets to block German tanks. Miron Białoszewski, a major Polish poet and a trenchant, obsessive memoirist of the Uprising, presumes to speak for "every average Varsovian" in maintaining that he preferred to live through the hell his city became in lieu of some "miraculous salvation outside of Warsaw." He attests that the first wooden barricades made of "tables, chairs, [and] wardrobes" were worthless, easily crushed under the tanks or burned down by shells, so "people started tearing up the concrete slabs from the sidewalks, the cobblestones from the streets. The tram drivers had prepared iron crowbars and pickaxes for this uprising. They handed them out to people. And with these the cobblestones were broken into pieces, the concrete slabs were dug up, the hard ground was broken."[8]

---

7 Rowińska, 1999, 75.
8 Miron Białoszewski, *A Memoir of the Warsaw Uprising,* trans. from the Polish and with an introduction and notes by Madeline G. Levine (New York: New York Review Books, 2014), 37, 7–8.

Figure 17. Street barricades constructed during the 1944 Warsaw Uprising at the intersection of Żytnia and Karolkowa Streets. Photographer: Stefan Bałuk. August 1, 1944. In the public domain.

Both civilians and fugitives came out to help in the heady early days of the Uprising. People ventured into the streets wherever the Germans were temporarily kept at bay. Zimmerman notes that "many of the 15,000–17,000 Jews residing in Warsaw emerged from hiding. These Jews shared the sense of euphoria that was palpable as civilians watched Polish insurgents with red and white armbands secure the streets and heard announcements declare the authority of the Republic of Poland."[9] In at least two cases, Home Army battalions freed Jews from deportation and internment. One of Kedyw Division's battalions, at Umschlagplatz, rescued fifty prisoners bound for the Treblinka death camp. On August 5, when the Zośka Battalion stumbled onto the Gęsiówka concentration camp located within the former Warsaw Ghetto, they used a captured tank to bash in its wall and freed 348 Jews, most of whom were foreign nationals.[10]

Krystyna knew that other Jews with false identities were serving in the Home Army, but she never realized that their numbers may have tallied in the thousands. At least five hundred formally participated in the Uprising, but it is impossible to ascertain how many acculturated Jews and Jews who had

---

9 Zimmerman, 2015, 385.
10 Ibid., 387, 391.

assumed Catholic surnames were involved.[11] The relations between Jews and Christians fighting in the Uprising were mutually supportive in the main, for all were bound by the common goals of routing the Germans and reclaiming Warsaw as the capital of a democratic, independent Poland. During these sixty-three days of open battle against the enemy, almost all the insurgents qualified and identified themselves as Polish patriots. Krystyna felt so safe with her comrades in the Home Army that she parted forever with her false identity as Zofia Łabędzka. As of August 1, 1944, she was once again Krystyna Bierzyńska, the native Varsovian fighting for her country at the tender age of sixteen.

Before Krystyna could enjoy the Uprising's initial euphoria, she had to endure her first and worst experience of the battle, while not quite in uniform. Before she joined her assigned battalion, she rushed home to pick up some supplies and say goodbye to Irena. Unfortunately, Krystyna's apartment building in Ochota stood just around the corner from German Army headquarters, a first major objective that the Home Army attacked and failed to occupy. As the Home Army soldiers hastily retreated, Krystyna's building, along with several others located in a square bounded by Wawelska, Plug, Mianowski, and Uniwersytecka Streets, was transformed into a fortress complex, absorbing men and women from different units and sheltering the wounded in their cellars. Over the next eleven days, those caught in this complex could hear the nearing sounds of the joint German–Ukrainian attack on the insurgents: shooting, grenade explosions, women screaming as soldiers raped them, and the thunderous report of a Goliath, a radio-controlled tank, which could destroy huge sections of a building.

This period of entrapment initiated Krystyna into the all-too-real Uprising of terror, death, and extreme physical exertion. In her besieged cellar, Krystyna and many others pledged their formal oath to the Home Army. Predictably, her initiation was eased by a good priest, Father Jan Salamucha, who gave absolution to the soldiers assembled there. Krystyna remembers his comforting words much more clearly than pledging the oath: "[Father Salamucha] talked individually with everyone who wanted to, and I told him that I'd never been so scared in my life. He told me that without fear there is no heroism, that you have to be afraid before you can be a hero. And he gave me strength."

As the apartment building above her was being bombarded into rubble, Krystyna and approximately sixty other Home Army members were forced to make use of Battleground-Warsaw's daunting safe passageways. Those who were healthy and able descended into a storm drain that supposedly would deliver them to the city center (Śródmieście), a district secured by the insurgents.

---

11 Ibid., 406.

A storm drain was preferable to a sewer, yet it was dark, claustrophobic, and small—a space in which a person could not stand up straight. Those using it had to proceed single file in a squatting position. Krystyna's group spent seven and a half hours inching their way forward, halting once as frightening rumors passed along the line about possible German detection and panicking at another point when someone was sure they smelled gas. Clearly these novice fighters were drawing on the frightening tales of the resistance in the Ghetto Uprising, when Jewish insurgents had resorted to sewers and storm drains as escape routes.

Despite their long ordeal, the sixty insurgents escaped with their lives. Those wounded soldiers who had remained in the makeshift fortress, including the comforting priest, were killed by the Germans. But before the lucky escapees could breathe easy in friendly territory, they encountered a last absurd obstacle, one akin to a famous funny scene in Andrzej Munk's classic film, *Bad Luck* [Zezowate szczęście] (1960). Munk depicts a clueless Polish soldier (played by actor Bogumił Kobiela) high-stepping his way through a cabbage patch as a German fighter plane bombards him. The juxtaposition of cabbages with near death points up the mundane surrealism of war. Krystyna's group likewise discovered how dangerous a cabbage patch could be. When the storm drain opened out to street level, they had to scramble onto Mokotów Field, a green open space that wartime residents had transformed into a vegetable garden. This space, in turn, was ringed by German machine gun posts and bright field lights. The sixty insurgents immediately discovered how loudly cabbage leaves squeaked when stepped on. They felt as if they were detonating vegetables. Luckily, no guards were listening or, for that matter, anticipating that a group of rebels would be emerging from below ground. Because the rebels appeared just before dawn, the field lights had been turned off and the natural light was still faint. Once the insurgents escaped the squeaking cabbage patch, they raced down several streets and over a barricade to safe ground in the city center.

KRYSTYNA JOINS THE UPRISING

In the city center at last, Krystyna reveled in being an accepted, even tested, participant in the Uprising. After collapsing on one of the mattresses stockpiled in what she thinks was either a school or hospital, she woke to temporary safety, freedom, and a decent meal. There Krystyna was ordered to enlist in the Iwo Battalion, since she had missed the date and place of her original posting. After nearly "two weeks of horror," her life became "euphoric and wonderful": "We sang, danced, marched around, and listened to music. We sang whenever we could unless we were told to be quiet because the Germans were around." The insurgents circulated an ever-growing number of songs being written about the Uprising, one of which starred "Małgorzata the Orderly"— the job Krystyna had been assigned. Along with the singing and dancing there was constant work to be done, but the general mood was ebullient, and social relations among so many young insurgents were free and easy, absent any parental control.

Thrilled to be fighting openly against the Germans along with so many other young patriots, Krystyna readily accepted her station as "flunky," carrying out whatever orders she received from her immediate superior. She wore no uniform. Only a red and white armband identified her as a member of the Home Army. Krystyna also carried an identity card, so that her relatives and friends could be informed somehow if she were killed. Otherwise, Krystyna's outfit evolved to suit her duties and included whatever useful item she could scavenge. She had entered the Uprising in a blouse and a skirt, which she later exchanged for a thin gray jumpsuit with long sleeves. On the piece of rope that she substituted for a belt, she hung a water canteen and a handy little leather ammunition case that some German soldier had left behind. Krystyna also carried a first aid bag, filled mainly with rolled bandages. For the most part, she and her fellow female orderlies lived in one set of clothes and rarely had the opportunity to wash their garments or themselves.

Figure 18. Patrol of Home Army female orderlies on Moniuszko Street. Photographer: Eugeniusz Lokajski. August 5, 1944. In the public domain.

Within the Iwo Battalion, Krystyna served as one member of a patrol—that is, as orderly and stretcher-bearer with three other young women. When Krystyna first told me about their strong-willed, steely patrol leader, Marysia Cegalska, I envisioned a professional woman in her forties. In fact, Cegalska was only nineteen, three years older than Krystyna. But she was disciplined and savvy enough to keep her team busy and useful.

Krystyna's patrol was never dispatched to the changing front lines of the Uprising. They remained in the city center for the duration, which turned out to be the district safest from bombing. Her patrol worked nonstop and on call. Krystyna remarked that she could not distinguish morning from evening, day from night in her memories because she did what she was told to do, and the orders never stopped. When her patrol did not need to pick up the wounded, they washed dishes and clothing, rolled bandages, put together first aid kits, and joined the assembly line to make *filipinki*, hand grenades filled with homemade explosives or explosives recovered from German shells. When food reserves dwindled later in the Uprising, she and other orderlies cooked soldiers big vats of what was dubbed "spit soup" (*spluwka*), so called because it consisted of wheat grain boiled in the husks that one had to spit out while eating.

Whenever there was military action, the patrols were immediately sent out to collect the wounded, one heavy body at a time. This work entailed navigating an ever more rugged and unrecognizable terrain, crawling over uneven piles of broken stone, cement, brick, metal, and other debris left by the bombing and shelling. The patrols functioned as the Home Army's makeshift equivalent to ambulances. Their job was straightforward and incredibly tough. Since medical specialists were scarce, no one was qualified to do triage, and all wounded needed to be recovered. Krystyna's description of a typical mission reflects its dogged grimness:

> We picked up [the wounded]. That was what we were there for. We carried the stretcher. I don't remember how far we walked, but we would scramble over the rubble until we saw someone who was wounded. We rolled him over onto the stretcher and tried to carry him. We were strong girls. Most of the time we brought the wounded to a cellar somewhere. There were no hospitals.

Due to the lack of supplies and the orderlies' elementary training in first aid, the patrol's efforts to treat the wounded were terribly limited. Using the water and bandages she carried, Krystyna would do her best to clean the soldier's wound, stop the bleeding, give him a sip of water, and wipe his face. She and the other orderlies had no access to morphine. The young women tried not to express horror or despair at the sight of their temporary charges, which was no easy task. "You get used to seeing blood," Krystyna told me. "But you don't get used to suffering." Indeed, when Krystyna's patrol helped carry out the wounded after the insurgents captured their largest objective, the tall Polish telecommunications building nicknamed PASTA, she took pity on one of the only German prisoners of war she encountered during the Uprising. A wounded middle-aged man in a Wehrmacht uniform lay calling for water, and Krystyna gave him a drink from her canteen. As she reasoned then, this man "could have had a daughter my age, and he didn't want to be there." The only sight that completely unnerved Krystyna during the Uprising was her discovery of a burned corpse as she was making her way through the cellars connecting different buildings. She has never been able to forget this image of a human being turned into charred flesh, tortured and killed by fire. Krystyna's patrol, like so many others, worked past the point of exhaustion as the fighting intensified. She cannot recall sleeping in a real bed after the night of July 31, 1944, the eve of the Uprising. During her seven long weeks of service, Krystyna slept whenever and wherever sleep was possible, lying down or sitting up. Though she did not endure the relentless bombing raids and the constant hunt for a sturdier cellar that Białoszewski describes with in-the-moment intensity in his *Memoir*, Krystyna knew the telltale sound of different German artillery and shared civilian Varsovians' fear of being buried alive.[12] Her patrol suffered a close call when a staircase under which they were sheltering partly collapsed, raising an enormous cloud of dust.

By the end of September 1944, it became clear that the insurgents could no longer sustain their battle with the Germans, for they were running out of weapons, ammunition, food, and water. Krystyna names hunger as her second worst ordeal during the Uprising, superseded only by the all-night passage through the storm drain and the mad scramble through a gun-ringed cabbage field. Even so, she understood how relatively lucky she had been when she witnessed other Home Army recruits in action. She remains awed by the "absolutely fearless" twelve-year-old boys, "the children of Warsaw," who were killed as they delivered messages and packages all over the city, constantly crossing enemy lines. When Krystyna caught sight of men in the Zośka Battalion emerging from the sewers after horrific fighting in the Old Town district, she was

---

12 Białoszewski, 2014, 87–90.

thunderstruck: "They looked terrible. So many of them had lost everybody. They were dirty, smelly, hungry, and bleeding. They were such heroes. And we were not."

At any time during the Uprising, Krystyna could have abandoned the Home Army and rejoined her civilian family. She alone of her new Warsaw family had chosen to fight, whatever her actual duties entailed. Krystyna certainly did not think less of Basia and Stefan for remaining civilians. The division between insurgents and civilians was not strictly drawn, particularly when it came to improvising defenses and recovering the wounded. After a skirmish or a bombing, civilian volunteers were often recruited to help fortify a shelter, dig out those buried in the rubble, or carry a stretcher. Krystyna also realized how much her family, like most civilians, was suffering from hunger. At one point, she managed to locate them in their current shelter and give them some of her food. They, in turn, begged her to stay with them because they worried about the dangers she faced out in the open. Given the fact that the German forces and their allied units shot, bombed, and burned soldiers and civilians alike, it was not at all clear who would be more protected once the Uprising inevitably failed.

BEING JEWISH IN THE UPRISING

Krystyna, like Dolek, had been baptized early in the war and later assumed a false identity for protection once she had relocated in Warsaw. Yet, unlike her brother, she witnessed no antisemitism in the Warsaw Resistance or during her service in the Home Army. Just as Krystyna had the great fortune to be adopted and cared for by a network of Gentile family friends and their children, so too she was lucky to find complete acceptance and support wherever she served and lived with the Home Army. Not all Jews in the Warsaw Uprising were so well-received. Whereas Krystyna felt safe enough in her new role as insurgent to "unmask," abandoning her fake name and identity, other Jews were warned by friendly Polish Christians to retain their cover stories "because of anti-Semitism in the Home Army."[13]

Zimmerman notes instances where Home Army commanders had to defend insurgents in their units who were exposed as Jews and appalling cases in which Jews were actually murdered by antisemitic Home Army soldiers. The numbers of those killed by fellow Poles in the Warsaw Uprising were few—30 out of an estimated 4,500 Jews who perished—but such atrocities reflected a

---

13 Zimmerman, 2015, 400.

phenomenon much more prevalent in northeastern Poland, where the Home Army incorporated extreme right-wing, antisemitic groups.[14] Relatively speaking, the Warsaw Uprising gave acculturated Jews the best odds to fight as one with Polish Catholics. This was certainly Krystyna's experience.

Nevertheless, Krystyna shared with other Jews in the Home Army a special impetus to fight, for the Germans had targeted her family for destruction, and had murdered her mother, grandmother, uncle, aunts, and cousins. As much as she loved her surrogate family, her real family's persecution by the Nazis and her own fiery character compelled her to action. Ever since Krystyna had returned to Warsaw, she had been able to abandon the debilitating survival strategies of patience and self-concealment. Back in her beloved big city and freer than ever to roam its streets, she was a rapidly maturing adolescent adept at "passing" and finding like-minded rebels in Warsaw's still diverse society. Once the Uprising began, she did not plan to sit it out in a cellar, praying for the danger to pass. As far as Krystyna knew, she no longer had any Jewish relatives whom her action might endanger. She intended to serve until the very end, even if that meant death. During the Uprising, Krystyna could not imagine her life beyond it.

Reviewing the testimonies of Jews who participated in the Uprising, Zimmerman remarks that many joined up not only for its feeling of openness and release, but also to exact revenge.[15] They shot at the Germans not to impress and sway Gentile observers with a "heroic death," as the Warsaw Ghetto fighters did in part. Rather, these Jewish insurgents wanted to even the score so as to avenge their loved ones and challenge the Nazis' racist worldview: Jewish lives taken would cost "Aryan" Germans their lives. Krystyna did not attempt to become a gun-touting heroine or a family avenger. Yet, she, too, was intent on proving her human worth, and, by extension, her family's human worth, by joining the Home Army in an open, more or less unified, rebellion against the Third Reich: "Oh, I wanted to be a part of it because when you're stepped on and destroyed and then suddenly you can show that you are worthwhile, it's freedom, it's air!"

Hundreds of thousands died in the Warsaw Uprising, the vast majority of them civilian Varsovians. But once a cease-fire was declared on October 1 and 2, 1944, and the Home Army formally capitulated on October 3, the insurgents did not face the same dreadful fate meted out to the Warsaw Ghetto fighters. The Soviet Army, which had parked itself on the other side of the Vistula River,

---

14 Ibid., 402, 404, 371–72, 406.
15 Ibid., 393. "A theme that recurs in Jewish testimonies is the wish to settle the score with the Germans. 'I accepted the Uprising,' Yitzhak Zuckerman recalled, 'with a feeling I can't put into words: a feeling that, at last, the moment of revenge on the Germans had arrived.'"

ordered by Stalin to render little to no assistance to the insurgents, expected the Germans to clean up the remnants of the Home Army; they would not need to arrest the Home Army officers themselves. But the Western Allies prevented either action, pressuring the Germans into recognizing the insurgents as prisoners of war under the terms of the Geneva Convention. By October 1944, the German military forces had realized their precarious position as they fought desperately on two fronts. In defeat, if not in battle, the Polish Home Army would be treated as the Allied forces were treated. They would be marched out of Warsaw alive and transported west to prisoner of war camps, not death camps or sites of slave labor.

When this agreement was reached, Krystyna recalls:

> It was clear that we could then decide to be with the civilians. All we had to do was take off our armbands and sit with them. So Basia and Stefan came to see me. They knew where I was, which was amazing. They begged me to go with them, wherever they were going to go, and I could leave! There was nothing stopping me. I remember Stefan begging me, repeating that "It is all over, Krysia" [Wszystko skończyło, Krysiu]. All of the civilians were being taken out ahead of us.

Krystyna's negative response to Stefan's pleas distinguished her from most of the Jewish insurgents, "who avoided being taken prisoners of war" for fear of exposure and execution.[16] It broke Krystyna's heart to say goodbye to Basia and Stefan, the "older siblings" whom she so loved and respected. Yet her experience in the Uprising had realigned her identity once more and, in her mind, would enable her reunion with Dolek, the most important person in her world. Unlike other Jewish insurgents, Krystyna completely trusted her co-combatants in the Home Army and felt both free and equal in their midst. As she explained to me:

> The worst that happened was that I was a prisoner of war. You know, I survived. I was safe! I was amongst others. I was protected. I was not running. I had my own name. When we were told that we had capitulated, one of the things I remember clearly is that we would be staying together, not walking away alone, one by one. Because there is safety in numbers. If you were alone, you could be killed and there would no record, nothing. So if you wanted to be safe, then you needed to be together with others.

---

16 Ibid., 409, 413.

Krystyna was convinced that traveling west safely ensconced among other prisoners of war would lead her to Dolek. She stubbornly repeated this belief as fact to Basia and Stefan as they tried to dissuade her: "I'm going west because Dolek is there. Dolek is in the west." She vehemently resisted her friends' attempts to advise and help her. It was as if the extreme exertion of the Uprising drove her to stay with her pack and be single-minded about her goal. It seems very likely that after seven weeks of trauma after trauma, exhausting work, constant fear and vigilance, little sleep, and ever less food, any insurgent would want to run away. As Krystyna pointed out to me, some insurgents had homes elsewhere to which they could retreat. Warsaw had provided her with a first home and, under dire circumstances, a second home, but in the wake of the Uprising, she had no home at all.

Thus, on October 4, 1944, Krystyna parted with her dear friends and began marching out of the city with her battalion. Rowińska, who was an officer in the Home Army, remembers a deliberately formal exit: "We considered ourselves soldiers and we wanted to keep this image, and so we marched in columns in military fashion, our heads held high."[17] Krystyna cannot recall exactly how they marched, but the spectacle of their meeting with the Germans impressed her as extraordinary. First, the Germans were playing no music—neither

Figure 19. Units of the Home Army leave Warsaw after capitulating to the Germans. October 1944. From Narodowe Archwum Cyfrowe. 21-223.

---

17 Rowińska (1999), 94.

popular, morale-boosting tunes nor triumphal classical pieces. As it turned out, their silence conveyed respect. Second, as the insurgents walked past the uniformed German forces, placing guns and grenades in the baskets set up for their disarmament, the enemy officers saluted them. The Home Army soldiers were not being hustled along like the bandits and hoodlums they were invariably reported to be in the German press. Instead, the army of the Third Reich was honoring the exhausted, starved, raggedly dressed insurgents as worthy opponents. Krystyna and her co-combatants did not know what awaited them at the end of their march, but this display of respect surprised and moved them.

As the insurgents made their way out of the city, the Polish crowds who stood to one side hailed them openly as heroes rather than defeated prisoners of war. These well-wishers paid no attention to the German guards. Krystyna vividly remembers this amazing reception:

> Civilians and peasants were lining up on our right. There was the road, then a ditch, and then these people standing there waving to us, crying, and throwing us apples and bread and sausage. At this point, I heard someone say, "if you want to get out, do it now. Jump into the ditch and you'll be fine." Some of the girls got away. And no one got shot. I don't think the Germans really cared. There were some Wehrmacht officers watching us. The people were throwing us bread. I got an apple or something. The Germans were telling them to go away, but the Poles kept coming back. They were *awed* by us!

The Germans' somber recognition of the insurgents as a brave fighting force, the Poles' celebration of them as national heroes—these rites of passage, combined with Krystyna's full acceptance by her fellow combatants, ennobled her wartime identity as a *powstaniec*, an insurgent in the most renowned Polish battle fought on Polish soil in World War II. She was justly proud of what she had endured and how she had served over sixty-three days of fierce fighting and incessant self-sacrifice. When Krystyna Bierzyńska walked out of Warsaw, she walked into perhaps the most sanctified pages of Polish history, at least as it was written in Western exile. After the war, the new Soviet-backed Polish government persecuted members of the Home Army and tarnished their reputation in toto as fascist collaborators.[18] In the West, however, when Krystyna identi-

---

18 Antony Polonsky, "The Complex Story of the Armia Krajowa" (a review of Joshua Zimmerman's *The Polish Underground and the Jews, 1939–1945*), *Yad Vashem Studies*, 210.

fied herself as a participant in the 1944 Warsaw Uprising, a *female* combatant, she was met with admiration and wonder. It was an identity that encompassed all that she had become—a resilient survivor and rebel, an ardent Polish patriot emulating her father's and brother's examples, and a native Varsovian whose heritage and multiple families, both acculturated Jewish and liberal Christian, qualified her to be an appropriate representative of a Warsaw that had flourished before the war.

Nevertheless, the insurgents' heroism came at the price of their army's objective. The Uprising designed to deliver Warsaw into the hands of the Polish government-in-exile was a tragic failure, resulting in the deaths of hundreds of thousands of residents and the occupiers' vengeful razing of the city. As Krystyna left Warsaw, the place where she had been born, loved, cocooned, indulged, educated, loved again, camouflaged, and accepted into the Resistance, she turned around and saw only destruction: "My city was in rubble. It was a mound of darkness, burning and smoking. There was nothing left." This was Krystyna's last view of Warsaw for twenty-three years, a vision of her country as post-apocalyptic ruin.

CHAPTER 9

A Polish Prisoner of War, 1944–1945

In October 1944, Krystyna Bierzyńska and approximately seventeen hundred other women left Warsaw as members of a defeated Home Army that would eventually be liberated by their victorious Allies to the west. To this day, Krystyna keenly feels this wartime bond, forged through conspiracy, guerrilla warfare, shared service, and subsequent imprisonment. When she returned to Warsaw in 2014 to commemorate the seventieth anniversary of the Warsaw Uprising, she looked forward to her reunion with her former battalion leader, the no-less-steely Marysia Cegalska.

The aftermath of the Uprising only reinforced Krystyna's sense of solidarity with this particular Polish group. She and her female co-combatants had to be accommodated by a German war machine totally unprepared to house thousands of female prisoners of war, an unprecedented phenomenon.[1] The Germans scrambled to outfit camp facilities for this influx, separating officers from enlisted women and dispersing them provisionally to different camps: Stalag XI B Fallingbostel, Stalag XI A Altengrabow Gross Lübars, Stalag 344 Lamsdorf, Stalag X B Sandbostel, and Stalag IV B Mühlberg-Lazaret Zetthain.[2] Krystyna was initially assigned to Sandbostel, where the women shared the facility with the male prisoners who had been interned there for most of the war. Eventually, all 1,728 Polish female prisoners of war were moved to Stalag VI C Oberlangen.

As Krystyna and her comrades-in-arms moved from camp to camp, they were subjected to humiliation by the German forces—nonlethal, far less extreme forms of the kind of degradation that the Nazi concentration camp

---

1 Wanda Broszkowska-Piklikiewicz, in the tenth anniversary booklet about the liberation of Oberlangen, *Światowy Zjazd Kobiet-Żolnierzy Armii Krajowej Powstania Warszawskiego, Byłych Jeńców Wojennego Obozu Oberlangen*, Warsaw, April 12, 2005, 15.
2 Ibid.

system violently inflicted on its prisoners. After spending several nights on the outskirts of a burning Warsaw, the female prisoners of war, called *akaczki* (derived from the Polish "Armia Krajowa"), were packed into cattle cars heading west. Each car had a tiny window and a garbage bin in the corner that served as the communal toilet. No one informed the women of their destination. When the train made very occasional stops, allowing the prisoners to stretch their legs or relieve themselves outside under guard, Krystyna first felt shamed. "We had to jump down from the railroad car," she remembers bitterly, "and a German stood there with a gun pointing at your rear end while you were peeing. That was the first time I felt horrible in a particularly humiliated way."

INTERNMENT AT SANDBOSTEL

Once the *akaczki* neared their first camp, they were unloaded for a longer period to be deloused and to take showers—a more humiliating and terrifying ordeal, since everyone knew that the Nazis used the term "showers" in the concentration camps to designate gas chambers. The notion of delousing also seemed sinister, since no one in the crowded cars was yet infested with lice. The actual procedures Krystyna and her group underwent were merely unpleasant and counterproductive. German female workers brushed some sort of delousing concoction ("horrible goop") on the prisoners' hair and shunted them into a huge warehouse that housed the showers. To the prisoners' relief, the showers were more or less what they were supposed to be. To their acute discomfort, all the *akaczki* had to strip in front of male German guards, who ogled them and kept up a mocking commentary on what they saw. "This," Krystyna declares, "was so demeaning. There were older women among us, some of whom had had mastectomies, and we young ones encircled them and shielded them with our bodies." Their stripping to shower also proved pointless. There was so little water and soap available that the women could neither wash nor rinse the goop from their hair, which, as they soon found out, carried just what it was intended to destroy. The "clean" female prisoners of war returned to the cattle cars louse-ridden, the victims of German inefficiency.

Such humiliations, Krystyna recognized, were a far cry from the extreme sufferings and mass murder that the Germans perpetrated in the concentration camps. But it was important that she endured these humiliations with a supportive, resourceful collective, fellow Poles who banded together literally in front of a threatening enemy. Indeed, Krystyna, a good-looking, fast-thinking girl, instantly emerged as a defender of the older women in her group. Here, she was not a Jew protected by sympathetic Poles, but a young Polish citizen protecting her older co-combatants. Belonging to and serving this Home Army collective automatically qualified Krystyna as a valiant Polish soldier for her compatriots elsewhere in the German camp system. In her experience, no Polish prisoner of war denounced others as Jews to the German authorities. As miserable as the conditions turned out to be in Sandbostel, her first POW camp located in northwestern Germany, Krystyna felt warmed by the cheers of male Polish prisoners who had stayed up half the night to welcome the incoming women: "They knew all about the Uprising, and they were waiting for us girls."

During their six weeks in Sandbostel, the *akaczki* received plenty of support from their male counterparts, who had been moved to accommodate the women into ever more cramped quarters with French, British, Belgian, and other European prisoners. The Polish men threw the newcomers food and notes over the high fences of barbed wire that separated them from the women's barracks. Because the female prisoners had just arrived and were not yet registered with the Red Cross, the men shared with them the contents of whatever packages that they received. According to Krystyna, the Polish men also made covert arrangements with the Germans to provide the *akaczki* with extra guards to prevent sexual assault. Krystyna recalls feeling well cared for by "these amazing guys" in Sandbostel.

Krystyna distinguished herself here and in her last POW camp, drawing on some of the advantages of having been educated as a "citizen of the world." The same linguistic ability and broadly European worldview that had enabled her, albeit temporarily, to be sheltered from Polish antisemitism in the 1930s now helped her cross the language boundary between Poles and other national groups. Many of the notes flying across the barbed wire fences were written in French, and Krystyna, itching to be useful, volunteered to translate them. Her translation work netted her a life-saving friend, a Belgian tailor who was enchanted by the efforts of his "petite soeur d'exile." When Krystyna came down with a severe case of bronchitis during the bitter winter of 1944, her Belgian friend sent her a can full of warm rice pudding and a long string with which she was to provide him with her measurements. Using his camp connections, the tailor procured bolts of a royal blue felt-like material and from this sewed Krystyna a battle jacket, pants, and a little folding cap. This attractive uniform replaced her utterly inadequate jumpsuit, kept her warm, and earned her the nickname "Krystyna the Blue." The Belgian made sure that someone took her picture in this beautiful blue suit, and he presented Krystyna with his own picture as a memento. Many years later, Krystyna sent copies of both photos to the Museum of the Warsaw Uprising in the Polish capital.

Figure 20. Photo of "Krystyna the Blue" in the uniform made for her at Sandbostel. From collection of Krystyna Bierzyńska Stamper; appears here as reproduced for the "Insurgents' Biographies" archived in the Museum of the Warsaw Uprising.

INTERNMENT AT OBERLANGEN

Krystyna's group, along with all the other Polish female prisoners of war, was transferred in mid-December 1944 to Oberlangen, which stood in the marshes and peat bogs near the German border with the Netherlands.[3] Oberlangen was a desolate place that had been condemned by the International Red Cross as unfit for human habitation.[4] The Germans had been using it to house Soviet prisoners of war, internees they notoriously mistreated and then simply evicted to make room for the huge group of *akaczki*. At Oberlangen, Krystyna once again put herself forward to serve—this time in response to a female guard's

---

3   The number 1,728 is repeated throughout the anniversary booklet on Oberlangen. The number 1,721 women, on the other hand, is reported by Irena Skrzyńska, in her "Zarys historii kobiet-jeńców wojennych żołnierzy AK internowanych po Powstaniu Warszawskim w obozie Oberlangen (stalag VIC)," http://www.polishresistance-ak.org/16%20Artykul.htm, accessed June 12, 2017.
4   Wanda Broszkowska-Piklikiewicz, 15.

request for a German translator in the camp kitchen. Krystyna realized that she could speak enough German to get by and consequently landed the coveted post of cook, a job about which she knew nothing. She and four other girls quickly learned how to make huge vats of soup out of rotten meat, wormy potatoes, and chard—a green Krystyna soon came to despise. They stirred the awful mixture with utensils resembling oars. Such work was infinitely better than cleaning the latrines, carrying excrement out to the freezing swamp. The stinking vats of soup kept their adjoining barracks warm, and the five of them ate relatively well, concentrating on the boiled meat. The entire camp subsisted on this diet of stew, bread, bitter chard, and watery tea.

Krystyna's relatively comfortable life in Oberlangen did not last long. At the end of December, she suffered an acute attack of appendicitis, which she survived thanks to the intervention of the POWs' commandant, Irena Mileska (code name "Jaga") and the exceptional skill of a German surgeon who had been shipped back from the Russian front after his leg was amputated.[5] While Krystyna passed in and out of consciousness from a high fever and tremendous pain, Jaga convinced the camp administration to transfer the girl to a decent civilian hospital by invoking the rules of the Geneva Convention. Krystyna reckons that the camp authorities decided to save her skin in order to save their own in the near future. At that time, the Battle of the Bulge was raging southwest of Oberlangen.

After the operation, Krystyna's German-language skills came in handy as she talked with the German nuns who nursed her. The sight of their white habits at first convinced her that she had died and gone to heaven. Apart from its happy ending, the most interesting thing about Krystyna's hospital trip was her opportunity to leave the camp's confines and to observe acts of normal decency among friends *and* enemies. Though the German soldiers had been ordered to mount an armed guard in her makeshift ambulance, the men laid down their weapons as soon as they closed the truck's back doors, covered Krystyna with one of their overcoats, and lifted up her stretcher in order to ease her over the bumps in the road. Before Krystyna was loaded into the truck, her Polish friends had used her wrapped body as a human postbox, tucking notes and Red Cross package foodstuffs and cigarettes beneath her sheets. Krystyna was in too much pain to be

---

5 In *Światowy Zjazd Kobiet-Żołnierzy*, Helena Dmochowska explains that "Jaga," Maria Irena Książek-Mileska (1908–1988), was a well-educated, experienced veteran of the Resistance and the Uprising. She organized Scouts and taught high school courses underground during the Occupation and, at the ripe old age of thirty-six, served as the main representative of the *akaczki* in her first and second POW camps (10).

aware of what her friends were doing at the time, but in retrospect she could only applaud their ingenuity. Some of the items she gave to the hospital staff once she was on the mend. The German surgeon who saved her life received the prized jar of Nescafe. In the meantime, Poles who worked as forced laborers on nearby German farms heard that a Polish girl from the camp was recuperating from surgery in the local hospital. These visitors came bearing sausages and onions for her to distribute back at the camp, and took away the women's notes to be mailed. Krystyna would play postbox one more time on her return trip.

During her last four months at Oberlangen, Krystyna developed an increasingly intimate, mutually supportive relationship with the other *akaczki*, both young and older. Jaga and other barracks officers, who hid their Home Army officer ranks from the Germans, maintained morale with discipline, routine, regular appeals for the greater good, and spiritual and intellectual mentoring. When POWs gave birth in Oberlangen's grim camp hospital, Jaga's announcement that their babies would be naked prompted hundreds of prisoners to fashion baby clothes, blankets, and diapers from whatever scraps of fabric they still possessed.[6] An Italian priest, a POW imported from another camp, ministered to what was presumed to be the women's exclusively Catholic religious needs. In addition, two female POWs, one an officer and the other a trained nurse, came up with the idea of receiving sanction as this priest's "confidantes." Their status empowered them to answer questions drawn from a box into which prisoners slipped anonymous notes about their fears and problems. This smart duo helped those suffering from trauma and depression and succeeded in limiting the number of suicide attempts in the camp.[7]

It was imperative to keep the POWS as busy as possible, given the lingering gray winter of 1945 and decreasing food supplies. When the female prisoners were not occupied with the camp duties of cleaning latrines or gathering fuel (brushwood in the forest and peat in the marshes), educators and artists among them filled the empty afternoon hours with lessons on history and foreign languages and workshops in crafting mosaics and sculptures. Professional performers in Oberlangen put on the sort of theatrical revue that had been wildly popular between the wars in Poland's big cities. Their show thrilled their fellow prisoners and impressed the camp brass. One of the "resident" performers was the famous film and cabaret actress, Helena Grossówna

---

6 Broszkowska notes that the camp hospital at Oberlangen housed two hundred wounded and nine newborns (15).
7 Ibid.

(1904–1994), who had served as a lieutenant in the Uprising. During the long months at Oberlangen, the officers among the POWs reiterated their soldiers' status as recognized prisoners of war, which guaranteed their relatively humane treatment. In the meantime, German camp authorities kept pressing the women to become forced laborers in the Reich. At one point, an alleged friend of Hitler visited Oberlangen with the aim of recruiting a women's legion to fight against the Soviet Army. Both efforts failed.

Among the more than seventeen hundred women in the camp, Krystyna grew closest to the youngest *akaczki*, who ranged in age from fourteen into their late teens.[8] When these girls performed their odious camp duties, they derived some pleasure from time spent outdoors. They attended lectures given by older co-combatants; Krystyna did so to keep up her French. But what the girls most loved to do was go over and over their recent dramatic adventures. "We talked about the Uprising endlessly," Krystyna remembers. "Where we were and what happened and who was killed and what we did. Some of it was sad, some of it was funny. We talked about what happened when they deloused us and that horrible shower experience. Remember that we were all young and crazy."

In retrospect, talking about their recent past was perhaps the least crazy thing Krystyna and her friends could have done. When I asked her if the girls ever swapped information about their lives before the Uprising, she told me that "that just was not part of the program." It may have been too painful to contemplate all that they had lost over the long term—family members, friends, homes, and the comforts of those homes. As young as these girls were, they had absorbed certain lessons from their time in the Resistance and the Home Army, and a certain kind of self-censorship—not mentioning one's Jewishness, for example—may have become automatic. Talking about the Uprising must have been therapeutic, for it enabled them to grieve together, to verify each other's nightmarish or seemingly hallucinated experiences, and to build a larger, more compelling narrative of what they had achieved, even though their battle had ended in defeat. Talking about the Uprising reinforced their legendary status as female insurgents. It also distracted them from a tedious, enervating present in prison camp, where they hoped to outlive the war before it starved them to death.

Krystyna's support group, which numbered about ten girls, talked almost as obsessively about their immediate postwar plans. Many of the young *akaczki* intended to return to Poland, especially if they had received letters and packages from surviving relatives back home. Krystyna herself had both a

---

8 Skrzyńska estimates that ninety-four prisoners of war were girls under the age of eighteen.

package and a heartwarming letter from Basia and Stefan. They wrote how much they loved her and how worried they were about her treatment as a prisoner of war. Yet Krystyna repeated to her camp friends what she had told Basia and Stefan in Warsaw: Once the war was over and she was liberated, she would set out to find Dolek. Krystyna's girlfriends did not know about Benio and Stefania and her days hiding in southern Poland, but they had learned a great deal about the remarkable Dolek—his good looks, doctor credentials, and service in a free Polish Army unit somewhere. For some reason, Krystyna presumed that Dolek was posted in England; she did not know that he was serving in the Anders Army on the European continent. Wherever he was, Krystyna never doubted that he was alive and that the two of them would move together into a vague, yet brighter future beyond Poland.

LIBERATION

During the German and Soviet invasions of Poland in September 1939, Polish fighting forces were scattered across Europe and the USSR. Some units escaped to France and England, and were incorporated into the British Army. Others were captured by the Germans and spent the next six years as prisoners of war. Those taken prisoner by the Soviet Army were either sent into the Gulag system as forced laborers or, in the case of over twenty thousand officers, grouped in special prisoner of war camps from which they were deported for mass execution in the spring of 1940. Once the USSR was invaded by Germany in June 1941, the luckiest surviving Polish officers and soldiers were able to enlist into General Anders's independent Polish army; other survivors were absorbed into the Soviet Army.

It was a stroke of great good fortune, therefore, when Oberlangen was liberated on April 12, 1945, by an armored division largely made up of Polish officers and soldiers who had fled or been deported from Poland in the first months of the war. At least one of the liberators, Leopold Terlicz-Witkowski, had suffered forced labor in Siberian exile.[9] By August 1944, this armored division had come under the command of General Stanisław Maczek on the Normandy beaches, where they were attached to the First Canadian Army's Second Corps.[10] Over the following months, Maczek's First Armored Division traveled east through France, Belgium, and Holland, helping liberate city after city on their way to Germany.

---

9 List Leopolda Terlicz-Witkowskiego, in *Światowy Zjazd Kobiet-Żołnierzy*, 20–21.
10 *Światowy Zjazd Kobiet-Żołnierzy*, 11-12.

En route to the Dutch village of Ter Apel, the division received news of a strongly fortified camp containing either Polish political prisoners or POWs just across the German border. Division commander Lieutenant Colonel Stanisław Koszutski did not have permission to risk his men's lives on German soil, but he feared that the German guards would murder all their Polish prisoners in lieu of attempting their evacuation, as had happened in other camps. On April 12, Koszutski opted to investigate the camp with a twelve-man scouting party equipped with weapons, a jeep, two cars, motorcycles, and a tank. The patrol also included a war correspondent. [11]

By early April, Krystyna and Oberlangen's many other POWs were much more preoccupied with food than execution. The Western Allies' attacks had cut German supply lines, and the women were starving as a result. During the last few weeks of their imprisonment, Krystyna remembers, she and her friends mainly slept, too weak to do much else. On the morning of April 12, she was startled out of her dozing state by the sounds of gunfire and women shouting. Rushing toward the camp entrance, Krystyna caught sight of an unknown motorcyclist, who drove straight for the watchtowers and shot the guard. A few seconds later, the tank lumbered up—"and the tank drove right through the gates and stopped and the gates were down and the tank was there and everybody was screaming, seventeen hundred of us! Mass hysteria and total mayhem!"

The women instantly realized that the scouting party was Polish, and the scouting party was overwhelmed to find Polish *women*, the heroines of the Warsaw Uprising, held captive in this run-down fortified camp. Krystyna, who still tears up as she tells the story, recalls how the motorcyclist dismounted after he shot the guard and began to shout and weep, while the women behind the barbed wire went crazy with joy. Terlicz-Witkowski, likely the second motorcyclist in the scouting party turned liberators, was caught up in the same whirlwind of emotions. In a letter commemorating the sixtieth anniversary of Oberlangen's liberation, he remembers how he and the *akaczki* rejoiced:

> The camp was free! "Girls" came running out of the barracks. You probably remember that feeling of happiness to this day! Words can't do justice to what the mood was like in the camp. Just a moment ago, you were

---

11 "Kobiety żołnierze AK—powstańcy w niewoli niemieckiej," edited by Maciej Janaszek-Seydlitz on the basis of reports by Witold Konecki, Stanisław Kopf, Jadwiga Kosuń Kwaśnik Badmajew, Janina Kulesza-Kurowska, Marek Ney-Krwawicz, Janina Skarzyńska, and Damian Tomczyk (2006). http://www.sppw1944.org/index.html?http://www.sppw1944.org/powstanie/kobiety_jency.html, accessed June 12, 2017.

"prisoners of war," and then God sent you the freedom you'd been waiting for, and it was just that freedom that made you so happy. It brought back my own memories of being freed in "Siberia." I got a letter that informed me that I was "amnestied" and freed from the camp, and the NKVD [Soviet secret police] commandant told me that "I could go wherever I wanted to because I was free!"[12]

Oberlangen historian Irena Skrzyńska delivers a more orderly report about the liberation, detailing shots exchanged and the German officials' formal surrender. But she, too, cannot resist the dramatic romance of Poles liberating Poles in German-occupied territory. In Skrzyńska's account, a pretty young POW dressed in an oversized soldier's coat rushed out to ask the scouting party their nationality. One of the soldiers cried in response: "We're Poles, Poles, dear miss! The First Armored Division, love!" Screaming, weeping, and jubilation erupted until Jaga called the entire camp to attention and the women of the Home Army fell into ranks for inspection.[13]

Yet now their inspection was carried out before admiring eyes of Polish soldiers, not German camp guards. One of Krystyna's fellow prisoners, Janka Szczepańska-Wścieklica, offers this impressionistic memory of female prisoners of war suddenly transformed into beloved, respected comrades in arms:

> And then the Polish flag is flying over the camp! The call sounds for inspection.... It reminds me of those hateful daily inspections in the rain and freezing cold.... No one will be counting us anymore! Our "trusted man"—a woman [Jaga]—gives her report to a Polish lieutenant before the altar adorned by Mary the Mother of God, [an altarpiece] masterfully etched out of a glass jar. The lieutenant says something in a voice muffled by emotion. They in Normandy... we in Warsaw... freedom... returning to Poland... happiness... mothers waiting... working to build a better world... the battle still lies before them... I can barely hear or see because my eyes are bedazzled with the brightness, the light, the white cherry trees in bloom.[14]

Krystyna initially basked in the joy of liberation. She went wild with happiness as the tank toppled the gates in Oberlangen, and then stood proudly at

---

12 *Światowy Zjazd Kobiet-Żołnierzy*, 12.
13 "Kobiety żołnierze AK—powstańcy w niewoli niemieckiej."
14 Janka Szczepańska-Wścieklica, "Pierwszy dzień wolności," *Światowy Zjazd Kobiet-Żołnierzy*, 40.

Figure 21. The liberation of Oberlangen by Polish forces. Narodowe Archiwum Cyfrowe, sygn. 37-339-1.

attention to be inspected by the Polish liberating forces. As the day wore on, Krystyna sat on the ground with her starving friends and devoured the sardines and evaporated milk that Maczek's First Armored Division had rustled up for the hungry women. Eating was first order of business for the prisoners, even though poorly prepared food brought on attacks of vomiting and diarrhea. Concerns for physical safety kept almost all the women within the camp walls until the war in Europe officially ended on May 8, 1945. Before their army's unconditional surrender, German snipers killed several former prisoners of war who ventured out into the countryside. A few weeks later, the *akaczki* were moved from Oberlangen to Niederlangen, a much cleaner camp outfitted with normal mattresses and ample bedding. The women immediately used the sheets to sew themselves new clothes. While at Niederlangen, Krystyna celebrated the end of the war by going AWOL one day, riding behind some obliging soldier on a motorcycle through the German marshes and forests, dizzy with speed and freedom.

CHAPTER 10

A Family Pact

The war's end did not disrupt Krystyna's close ties with her co-combatants. Her service in the Home Army and her friendships with other female veterans shape her self-image to this day. Yet Krystyna did not share the bright vision of repatriation that her fellow POW Szczepańska-Wścieklica imagined—the waiting mothers, the blooming cherry trees. Krystyna's mother had been shot or gassed by the Nazis as a Jew betrayed by a Pole. And the hometown Krystyna loved and knew so well lay in ruins, bombed and torched by the German Army. Through her actions and ordeals, Krystyna had proved herself to be an ardent Polish patriot. But she could not conceive of what it would mean to return to a country buried under corpses and rubble, poisoned by the targeted murders of her Jewish relatives, and estranged by the unfriendly politics of the Soviet liberators. Krystyna would learn soon enough that a Soviet-aligned Poland would admit neither her nor her brand of patriotism.

Instead, Krystyna invested her energy in searching for the one person who could anchor her past, present, and future home. She began looking for her brother Dolek the very day that Oberlangen was liberated. Maczek's First Armored Division had dispatched doctors and ambulances to bear away the camp's wounded and mothers with newborns. Spotting this cluster of medical personnel, Krystyna marched up to a Polish officer whose red velvet badge identified him as a physician. She asked him if he knew a Dr. Adolf Bierzyński and would not take no for an answer. Fortunately, the officer she had accosted was patient and resourceful: "This doctor gave me a little booklet with all the different names of Polish organizations. He gave me a piece of paper and something to write with. Right then or maybe that night I wrote to the Scholarly Circle [*Koło Naukowe*] in London."

Krystyna realizes now how naïve she must have seemed, presuming that every army doctor would know her brother. Yet her action was smart and brave. It would have taken Dolek much longer to locate her. The last letter he had received from the family told him only that they had retreated to Zabierzów and his father "was away." Dolek might never have guessed that his baby sister had run off to join the Uprising and ended up in the lone female prisoner of war camp in Europe. As their interactions subsequently showed, Dolek did not anticipate what a confident rebel Krystyna had become. The very fact that Krystyna had initiated the search for her much older brother reflected her extraordinary gumption and independence, attributes honed by almost three years in the Polish Resistance.

Krystyna's letter eventually reached Dolek through the good offices of a Professor Gergovich in London, whose enquiries quickly located a Dr. Adolf Bierzyński in the Second Polish Corps then camped in Italy. Krystyna has kept the miracle of Gergovich's reply. When Krystyna tore open the envelope

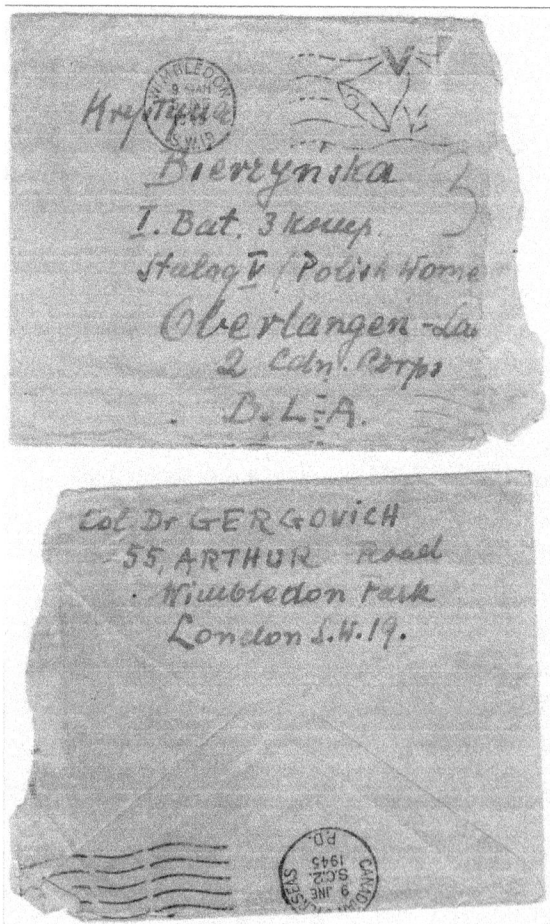

Figure 22. Photocopy of envelope from Professor Gergovich to Krystyna. From collection of Krystyna Bierzyńska Stamper.

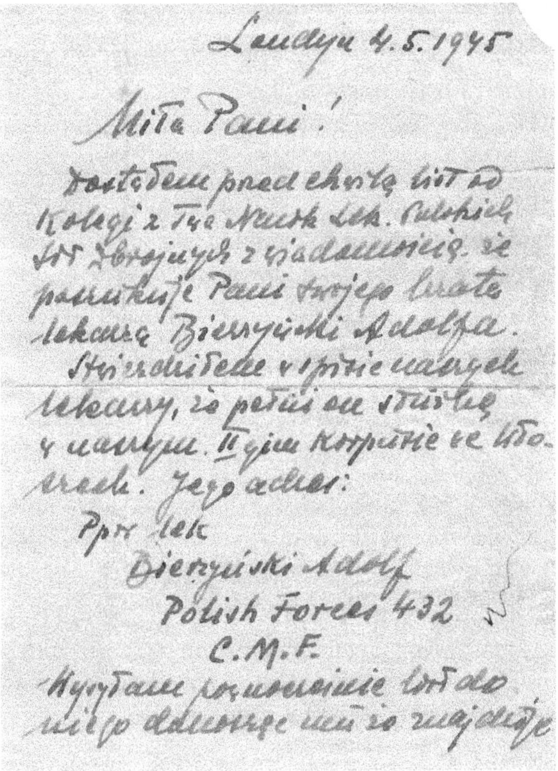

A Family Pact • CHAPTER 10 | 97

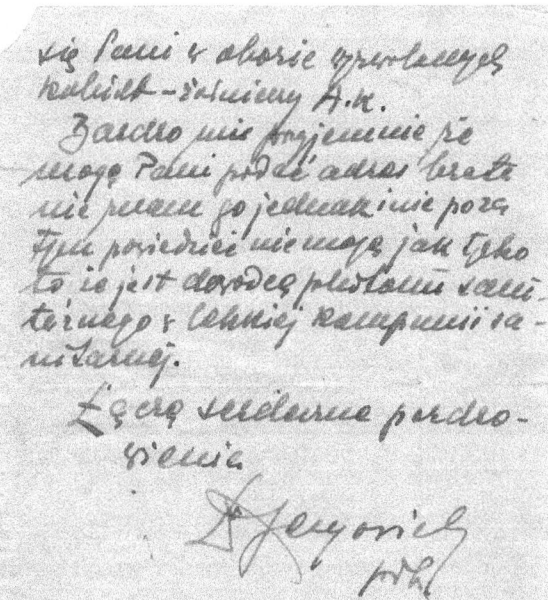

Figure 23. Photocopy of letter from Professor Gergovich to Krystyna. First page. From the collection of Krystyna Bierzyńska Stamper.

Figure 24. Photocopy of letter from Professor Gergovich to Krystyna. Second page. From the collection of Krystyna Bierzyńska Stamper.

stamped with the ominous Oberlangen address, the prison where she nearly died, she discovered her brother's mailing address and the treasured information that he was alive and not terribly far away.

Krystyna wrote to Dolek as soon as she had his address. His quick response thrilled her—he was overjoyed that she had survived—yet his instructions to her to stay put while he figured out the next steps infuriated her. The now seventeen-year-old Warsaw Uprising veteran had no intention of cooling her heels in Niederlangen after months in prison: "I got angry because I was ready to go!" When a ride out of Niederlangen materialized, Krystyna took it, hell-bent on reaching Dolek under her own power.

Though Dolek might have expected his sister to have inherited the Bierzyński hotheadedness, he did not reckon on Krystyna's courage in navigating the real world. Posted in Italy, Dolek did not have permission to drive to Germany, so he had to bend some rules to plot his trip. With unofficial help from a major whose daughter was interned with Krystyna and, unbeknownst to Dolek, was Krystyna's good friend, Dolek procured both a truck and an experienced driver to make the long journey north. But when Dolek and his driver finally reached Niederlangen, the only woman missing from the camp's roster of residents was Krystyna. The Bierzyński siblings had passed each other on the road.

This comedy of errors ended in a few days, after Krystyna heard that her brother was en route and she settled down to wait for his arrival. By this time, Dolek had formed a clearer impression of his sister's experience and cohort. At Niederlangen, he discovered that Krystyna's ten best friends, including the major's daughter, instantly recognized him from his sister's oft-repeated description of her handsome big brother, the important army doctor. All the young women insisted that Dolek, whom they considered practically family, should give them a ride to the II Corps's camp in Italy. They were only a bit less audacious than Krystyna. Dolek could not say no, though he made sure that these girls, unlike his sister, took their official leave from camp. When Dolek finally found Krystyna, he was forewarned, if not wholly prepared. Somehow the ten-year-old girl he had left behind in their parents' apartment on September 6, 1939, had grown up into a gutsy soldier, perhaps the boldest, most impetuous member of an all-female army unit.

Once sister and brother laid eyes on each other, they realized they had to dispense with the idealized image of the sibling they had enshrined in memory. Dolek was stunned to see how big Krystyna was, and Krystyna was surprised that her big brother no longer seemed quite as tall and god-like. They knew then that they both had many war stories to share and shocks to absorb.

The morning after Dolek's arrival, the Bierzyński siblings separated themselves from their traveling party and walked out to a little pond, beside which they spent the day talking and sometimes weeping.

DOLEK'S STORY

Dolek first talked about his terrible ordeal in Soviet captivity and escape into the Anders Army. His long trek through the Soviet Union and the Middle East comprised another painful, complicated, astonishing chapter of Poland's wartime history.

Dolek's military service on Polish soil had ended almost as soon as it had begun, as German and Soviet forces invaded Poland in September 1939 from the west and east under the terms of the Molotov-Ribbentrop Pact. The Soviet Army captured Dolek and thousands of his fellow officers and shipped them deep into the Soviet Russian and Ukrainian republics to prisoner of war camps being readied especially for this contingent of the Polish Army. Dolek ended up in Starobelsk, a camp located outside of the Ukrainian city of Kharkov.

At the outset, internment in Starobelsk under the Soviets might have seemed the lesser of two evils for Dolek. Despite his formal conversion to Christianity, Polonized surname, and officer rank as an army doctor, Dolek could have been exposed and immediately executed as a Jew by the Nazis in the west. Yet Starobelsk turned out to be a deadly destination. By March 1940, Stalin and his Politburo had approved a plan to round up and liquidate tens of thousands of Polish military and civilian leaders so as to ensure a much-weakened Polish state after the war. Dolek got word of this secret plan by accident, while he, a prisoner, was assigned to treat Soviet camp guards who had contracted venereal diseases or were injured in drunken brawls. One such patient, an inebriated secret policeman, boasted to his Polish doctor that "your fucking Poland will disappear just like all the rest of you!" Dolek did not understand just what this boast meant. But the slap he gave the prisoner in response and the ten-year labor camp sentence resulting from that slap saved his life. While the roughly four thousand prisoners in Starobelsk were sent off for mass execution in April 1940, Dolek was being transported to the far north, near the city of Kotlas, where he was consigned to forced labor until the Germans invaded the Soviet Union in June 1941.

In that camp, Dolek shared the sufferings of hundreds of thousands of Polish citizens who had been removed from the nation's eastern territories, or *Kresy* (borderlands), during the 1939–1941 Soviet occupation. Targeted as "class enemies" or picked up at random by the NKVD (the Soviet secret police), these people were deported by cattle car to cut trees in Siberia, labor on collective farms in Central Asia, or perish working in the gold mines of Kolyma in the Far East. Almost half of the estimated 500,000 deportees died of starvation, disease, and extreme cold, or were killed in secret executions.[1] Dolek's hard life in the logging camp near Kotlas closely resembled that of Stefan Waydenfeld and his deported family, who also felled trees in a camp near that city.[2] Waydenfeld's acculturated Jewish family endured high work quotas, inadequate rations, terrible cold, fierce blizzards in which laborers went missing, and short summers during which clouds of stinging, bloodsucking insects plagued the loggers.

Like the interned Waydenfelds, Dolek received "amnesty" from the Soviet government once Hitler unleashed his army against the USSR on June 22, 1941. The Molotov-Ribbentrop pact had been violated, and Soviet troops, taken by surprise, were pushed back in a chaotic retreat. Within months of the invasion, the Stalinist government was pressed to release its Polish prisoners for military duty. Surviving Polish deportees were now considered allies rather than enemy aliens and were allowed, with some restrictions, to join an independent Polish army being formed in the Russian towns of Buzuluk, Totskoe, and Tatishchevo, in a region near the Kazakh Republic. Dolek, along with three hundred men from his camp, began the long journey southeast to that region in autumn 1941, just as the cold weather set in. When night overtook the men, they attempted to survive the cold by sleeping in a kind of human ball they called a ślimak (snail). Each morning they drew straws for their nighttime positions. Those fated to sleep in the snail's outer shell usually froze to death. Dolek proved to be another resilient, extremely lucky Bierzyński. He was one of the few to survive the terrible three-month trek to Buzuluk, reporting for duty emaciated, but alive.

In Buzuluk, Dolek's qualifications as a Polish officer and a trained doctor worked to his advantage. He was admitted straightaway into the army under General Władysław Anders's command and put to work treating the many ailing civilians seeking shelter, food, and safety near the recruiting centers. Any suspicion of Dolek's Jewishness by the Anders admission officers might have been irrelevant since, according to historian Harvey Sarner, 60 percent of the army's doctors were Jewish, roughly the same percentage of Jews as in the medical profession in prewar Poland.[3] Dolek formed close friendships with other

---

1 Antony Polonsky, *The Jews in Poland and Russia*, vol. 3: *1914–2008* (Oxford: Littman Library of Jewish Civilization, 2012), 380–84.
2 Stefan Waydenfeld, *The Ice Road: An Epic Journey from the Stalinist Camps to Freedom* (Los Angeles: Aquila Polonica, 2011).
3 Yisrael Gutman, "Jews in General Anders' Army in the Soviet Union," *Yad Vashem Studies*,

Anders Army medical personnel, including a Doctor Różycki, who was also Jewish.

Of course, Dolek did not advertise his Jewish heritage, abiding by a policy of "don't ask, don't tell" similar to what Krystyna observed in wartime Warsaw. There were many high-ranking regular army officers who had been right-wing National Democrats before the war, members of a party notorious for its antisemitic stance. Anders himself was one. This did not mean that all such officers were antisemites. But the relationship between the admitting officers and those noncommissioned recruits who identified themselves as Jews was contentious, to say the very least. Given that Jews made up 10 percent of the Polish population, only a proportionately low number of openly Jewish soldiers (5 to 6 percent) were let into the army for an array of reasons—blatant antisemitism, generalized misperceptions of all Jews preferring Soviet communism to Polish nationalism, and prejudices held by Allied officers the world over that Jews would make poor soldiers.[4]

Figure 25. Dr. Adolf (Dolek) Bierzyński in uniform of the Polish II Corps. From collection of Krystyna Bierzyńska Stamper.

Despite the ameliorating presence of some liberal Polish officers who treated Jewish recruits fairly and encouraged their efforts, Jewish soldiers encountered the worst manifestations of antisemitism during the army's terrible months in the Soviet Union. These soldiers' situation only improved once the Anders Army was evacuated to British-held Iran and was formally attached as the II Corps to the British Eighth Army in spring 1942. During the II Corp's

---

vol. 12 (Jerusalem: Yad Vashem, 1977), 231–96; Harvey Sarner, *General Anders and the Soldiers of the Second Polish Corps* (Cathedral City, CA: Brunswick Press, 1997), 143.
4 Sarner, 1997, 94, 96, 102.

extended stay in Mandate Palestine, where they were welcomed by an affluent, powerful Jewish community, approximately 3,000 of the 4,300 Jewish soldiers in the II Corps decided to desert or, in a few cases, obtain an honorable discharge. Some reenlisted in the British Eighth Army proper, some dispersed to work in the local kibbutzim, and some committed to serve in the covert operations of Irgun, the Zionist paramilitary operation fighting for the establishment of an independent Jewish state.

But Dolek was not tempted to desert. Like most of the acculturated Jews who passed for Polish in the II Corps, he remained with the army for the duration of its existence. As Sarner observes:

> The low percentage of deserters among doctors may be attributed to their officer rank, which shielded them from the whims of malicious officers or NCOs with anti-Semitic prejudices. In addition, soldiers going into combat would not want to offend a doctor whom they might meet later in an operating room. The overriding consideration which kept doctors from deserting was their professionalism: they felt the Polish Army needed them and even if they were not sure whether they would want to return to Poland after the war, they still felt an obligation to it as doctors, if not as Polish citizens.[5]

Dolek faithfully served in the II Corps as it traveled through Iran, Iraq, Syria, Mandate Palestine, and Egypt from spring 1942 until early 1944. It then shipped out, at last a physically fit and well-trained fighting force, to join the Western Allies in the Italian campaign. In the Corps' first major action, the battle to capture the mountaintop objective of Monte Cassino, once a monastery and now a German-held fortress, this branch of the Polish Army demonstrated its grit and valor in fierce combat. Dolek and his friend Różycki distinguished themselves as exceptional officers, army doctors who rushed to aid the severely wounded under their charge. Both were attached to a tank unit, the Third Squadron of the Fourth Armored Division. As Zbigniew Wawer reports in his detailed history, *Monte Cassino 1944*, the Third Squadron suffered a hellish attack from German artillery on May 12, 1944. As the US-made tanks moved in to support the Polish infantry:

> Volleys of mines and crashes of ammunition tore open the steel seams of the Sherman tanks and all those inside were killed or horribly burned.

---

5 Sarner, 1997, 143.

Doctors Różycki and Bierzyński arrived before dark to carry out their duties, even though they themselves were wounded.[6]

For his actions, Dolek was awarded the *Virtuti Militari*, Poland's highest military decoration for heroism and courage, equal in stature to the US Medal of Honor and the British Victoria Cross. It bears noting that, among the remaining thousand identified Jewish soldiers in the II Corps, an impressive 118 were "decorated for honorable action, courage, and bravery" in European battles by January 1945. Identified or camouflaged, many Jewish soldiers and officers proved to be the excellent warriors that career officers in the Polish Army had deemed them incapable of becoming.

KRYSTYNA'S STORY

Krystyna had a great deal to tell Dolek, too, as they sat by that little pond in Germany. Dolek had already guessed about Benio's death from his mother's cryptic postcard: "Papa was sick. He's not here right now." Dolek had anticipated his father's cancer diagnosis, since Benio's symptoms had appeared before the German invasion. Yet Dolek was caught unawares by news of simpler, smaller misfortunes. When Krystyna told him how the family temporarily lost their dog Żabka and found her eating garbage in their building's courtyard after the September 1939 bombardments, Dolek broke down: "That's when he cried. This explained everything. If Żabka was eating garbage, then our old life was over. We held each other and he cried."

Dolek could never make peace with the fact that their mother had vanished: "My brother was incredibly close to my mother. And she adored him. He was the light of her life. He thought it was so horribly unfair that she was gone and we really didn't know what had happened." Stefania's capture and killing dealt the most painful, complicated psychological blow to her children. Krystyna felt keenly that Stefania should not have endangered herself and left her daughter an orphan. Dolek railed against the injustice of his mother's complete liquidation. Stefania was the lone member of their nuclear family to be murdered. This amazingly capable, intelligent Jewish woman, the rescuer of her mother-in-law, sister, and daughter, failed just once to pass as an Aryan. Stefania's death proved to Krystyna and Dolek that no Jew, however acculturated and clever, could have been invincible in Nazi-occupied Poland. Their survival was a fluke, not the consequence of being Warsaw Bierzyńskis.

---

6   Zbigniew Wawer, *Monte Cassino 1944* (Warsaw: Bellona, 2009), 171-72.

While Dolek agonized over Stefania's disappearance, he was astounded by his little sister's war record. Krystyna summed up the force of his response in a pithy sentence: "He was very proud of me forever." Dolek was fascinated with her stories about the Uprising. They inspired him to become her first biographer. When Krystyna visited him and his family after the war, Dolek made home movies in which he interviewed his sister about her experience in the Uprising and the POW camps. He insisted that his children watch them and remember. Twenty-five years after his death, Dolek's daughters continue to tell Krystyna that "Daddy said that Auntie Christine can do no wrong." The bearer of the *Virtuti Militari* recognized his little sister as a war hero in her own right.

That quiet spring day in Germany, Krystyna and Dolek began a conversation that amplified and deepened their relationship for decades to come. They remembered and mourned their parents, aunts, uncles, cousins, and friends—the most important people in their prewar life. Dolek surely learned of the Nazis' campaign to annihilate the Jews as he was traveling through the Middle East. He likely read news of the Warsaw Ghetto Uprising when he was in Mandate Palestine; the Polish-language newspapers distributed to the II Corps reported about the insurgents' bravery and their terrible end. But now Dolek had to absorb Krystyna's personal account—what she observed or guessed—about his family members' individual deaths. Though Dolek, like Krystyna, had persisted in believing that his sibling had survived, he had no way of anticipating how that would happen—how far-sighted, self-possessed, and resourceful their parents would be in escaping Nazi persecution for several crucial years and keeping his sister safe. Nor did Dolek have any idea of how the Nazis hunted down his aunt and grandmother and murdered them on a hillside, or how his other close relatives perished in the Warsaw Ghetto, struck down by typhus or engulfed in flames and smoke during the Ghetto Uprising.

It was during this day of sharing and mourning, Krystyna told me, that she and Dolek decided not to talk about being Jewish—more, that they did not want to talk about it. When I pressed her about this decision, wondering if Dolek had felt proud of being Jewish when he was stationed in Mandate Palestine, Krystyna's response was bitter and emphatic:

> No, no. Remember, his being a Jew was never up front, or he would not have been admitted into the Anders Army. He could not go to medical school, so why would he be proud? And he told me that nobody in the army knew. Mum was the word. We didn't talk about it. It didn't do us any good. Look, we decided, brother and sister, that that was it.

The pact that Dolek and Krystyna made that day obviously unraveled over the ensuing decades. Krystyna told her children about their shared Jewish heritage when they were old enough to understand, and was buoyed up by their pride and excitement. Years before she met me, she had consented to be interviewed as a survivor of the Shoah. She mailed me a DVD of the interview as a first introduction to her war. Krystyna devoted days on end to our interviews, during which she reflected on her Jewishness in prewar and wartime Poland.

Yet I understand, I think, why Krystyna and Dolek resolved on this silence right after the war. It is one thing to embrace your Jewish heritage in late twentieth-century America, in a time and place where multiculturalism is more the rule than the exception and ethnic and religious tolerance is generally supported. Mandate Palestine, with its assorted emigrant communities and cultures, is no more, replaced by the strong, independent state of Israel. The Holocaust perpetrated by the Nazis has come to be denounced (almost) globally as one of the greatest crimes against humanity. There now exist many models of explicitly Jewish agency and heroism, unearthed from a past long obscured by nationalist narratives or pioneered since World War II in response to the horrors of the Holocaust and Israel's fierce struggle to survive in the Arab world.

In the spring of 1945, however, Krystyna and Dolek knew no such role models—with the exception, perhaps, of the Jews who chose to die fighting in the Warsaw Ghetto Uprising. The brother and sister's survival depended on masking their identity as Polish citizens of Jewish heritage. Their heroism consequently figured as undifferentiated Polish Catholic heroism, the personae they had assumed before enlisting in their respective armies. Dolek knew that Polish Jewish officers and soldiers were eventually distinguished for their valor during the European campaign. The II Corps tombstones in the military cemetery of Monte Cassino would bear Stars of David as well as crosses. But such a distinction was a very recent, fragile phenomenon, encouraged mainly by the religious pluralism encoded in the practices of the larger British Allied force to which the II Corps was attached. Krystyna had grown used to the absolute necessity of passing as an Aryan because she had lived under the Nazi occupation for six years. Her experience had taught her that neither Jews nor Catholics wanted to raise the topic, because everyone craved the safety and simplicity of being classified as Polish resisters and soldiers. The Bierzyński siblings' Jewishness "did them no good" not because they were ashamed of it, but because their successive contexts each targeted it for attack.

This implied demand for self-censorship meant that Krystyna and Dolek would have to go on living with masks in place, even after the Nazis were defeated. And though their stories, told together, encompass much of Poland's wartime history within and outside of the nation, they would not be able to tell them fully and freely for many years. During the war, Polish nationalism, the presumed religious and ethnic homogeneity of the "we," forced Polish Jews to maintain the right "look," to champion the right "national" sociocultural values, to keep silent about their families, and to hide their unmentionable traumas from their comrades-in-arms even as they risked their lives for Poland.

As Krystyna and Dolek began to piece together their adult relationship and postwar lives, they also realized that they could not afford to dwell on this incessant injustice and allow it to warp their futures. They decided not to return to Poland after the war, where the Holocaust had rendered Jewishness even more alien and Catholicism and ethnic Polishness the norm. Warsaw would rise again, but it could never recreate its existence as a Jewish metropolis, the nation's most promising incubator for multiculturalism. As prewar Varsovians, Krystyna and Dolek had been raised to be the first citizens of what their Jewish parents hoped would become a progressive, pluralistic state. After the war and the demobilization of the Anders Army in 1946, they sought that state elsewhere. Krystyna eventually settled in the United States, and Dolek found refuge working as a doctor on the Caribbean island of Grenada, where he would never again experience the killing cold of Russia.

Figure 26. Photo of Dolek and Krystyna taken several decades after the war. From collection of Krystyna Bierzyńska Stamper.

CHAPTER 11

Krystyna Bierzyńska in Polish History

When I first suggested to Krystyna Bierzyńska that I write about her Warsaw childhood and war-torn adolescence, she balked. Though she was proud to have served in the Home Army, a distinction that brought her back to Poland several times for state-celebrated reunions, she doubted that her experience would be of much interest to American readers. In Krystyna's estimation, she simply did not qualify as an interesting, sufficiently heroic protagonist. She had not suffered the indescribable tortures of the concentration camps. Nor had she acquitted herself as a brave fighter trudging through the sewers and shooting at German soldiers from Warsaw's crumbling walls and abandoned buildings. Unlike her older brother Dolek, the commissioned officer in uniform, Krystyna had not been awarded Poland's *Virtuti Militari*.

With the benefit of hindsight, I think Krystyna also vacillated over my proposal because she has made her story part of a vital collaborative project, interweaving it with the stories of those whose experience intermittently intersected with hers. Through letters, phone calls, visits, and eventually email and Skype with family and old friends, Krystyna constantly relives and revises her story. For example, when she could not remember exactly when her paternal grandfather died and how her father emerged as the head of the family, she called her cousin Marysia, Henryk's daughter, and swapped memories. When Krystyna wanted to know where and how her unit slept after they were marched out of a burning Warsaw in 1944, she double-checked with a surviving co-combatant and, while on a trip to Warsaw, she hired a cab and had the driver retrace their route and clock the kilometers they walked. That Krystyna has maintained contact with so many of the people she met before and during the war is both a stroke of exceptional good luck and a testament to her enormous gift for friendship. The cohort she formed at Oberlangen is modest compared with the global community she has cultivated over the decades—both relatives and their descendants and co-combatants and their descendants scattered the world over, from Poland to Australia. While Krystyna lives, the story of her childhood and war is in constant circulation: shared, compared, and referenced; used to remember and savor the characters of lost family and friends; and riveting ever more listeners through her passionate storytelling and great personal warmth.

This book, alas, cannot drop readers literally into Krystyna's dining room, where they could admire her grandmother Gustawa Neufeld's portrait and enjoy the great privilege I had of listening to her. Instead, I have framed Krystyna's uncensored story in its changing contexts in order to integrate it into a more individually textured, multicultural history of Poland and the Jews of Poland. In 1945, Krystyna faced a much more difficult dilemma—risking her life rather than writing her past from a safe geographical and temporal distance. She decided that returning to Poland and going public with her Polish Jewish identity would be too painful and too dangerous. After all, the "country" in which she had been raised, Poland's most heterogeneous metropolis, lay in ruins after a coalition of Varsovians fought to liberate it. To this day, Warsaw is usually remembered around the world as a city destroyed—an infamous site of the Holocaust and the battlefield for two major devastating uprisings. Its dead residents have been buried in popular history under simplistically separated nationalist categories, as Polish and Jewish victims and Polish and (far less commemorated) Jewish insurgents.

As Krystyna's story demonstrates again and again, such nationalist stereotyping diminishes who she is and ignores the startling, sometimes contradictory composite of her experiences and perceptions. Krystyna was neither an Orthodox Jew nor a completely assimilated Jew. She was neither a Jewish partisan who resisted contact with "inevitably" antisemitic Poles nor a Jewish victim who utterly depended on "angelic" Polish Christian saviors. Indeed, Krystyna was not even consistent in her animosity toward the Germans, for she recognized instances of German suffering and empathy during the Uprising and the hard months in the POW camps. Krystyna's Jewishness did not predetermine her roles and allegiances, but made her keenly aware of other people's complexity and accepting of their differences.

Moreover, Krystyna understands, as have many Polish citizens of her generation, how difficult it is to explain her war to those who experienced it on the other side of the ocean or the Channel, or in countries where the Germans treated the conquered as enemies but not subhumans and where the Soviet Army remained a comfortably remote ally. The Polish writer Tadeusz Konwicki

(1926–2015), who also matured during World War II but served in the Home Army as a partisan far from Warsaw, struggled his whole life to articulate a coherent identity, for his had been battered early on by calamity after calamity. In a 1991 interview with Dorota Sobieska, Konwicki argued that a history of his generation has to join the idiosyncratic extremes each individual has endured:

> The point is that my generation is aware of its fate all at once. There is no way to forget the whole biography and no way to avoid saying about that man eating a hard-boiled egg that he had been in Auschwitz or that this woman, so well-dressed and perfumed with Chanel, survived a Siberian labor camp.... I mean biographies with war, ideological changes, crucial questions, constant wrestling with the ultimate, which an American middle-class man never faces.[1]

Krystyna Bierzyńska's story serves as an excellent case in point, a key part of a "whole biography" of idiosyncratic extremes that must be inscribed in the branching, tangled narratives of twentieth-century Polish and Polish Jewish history. When I first met Krystyna, a good-looking, outgoing woman in sunny Southern California, I could not guess the calamities she had suffered or the dangerous, heroic feats she had risked in her youth. Though I knew she had participated in the 1944 Warsaw Uprising, I could not have predicted her dive into the Resistance as a fourteen-year-old girl or imagined her service as a teenage orderly scrambling over rubble to bear the wounded away. I could not have envisioned her stirring huge vats of soup for some seventeen hundred women insurgents in a prisoner of war camp.

Krystyna's Jewishness further complicates the startling link between peacetime normalcy and wartime extremity that Konwicki identifies as a hallmark of his generation. Krystyna's survival is certainly all the more remarkable because of it. Yet her Jewish heritage also cements her bond with a multifaceted Warsaw that most historians have not yet fully appreciated. Krystyna grew up in one of the very few places in interwar Poland that incorporated her difference and offered her exceptional opportunities. Her parents' complementary upper-class lifestyles and her cocooned and then carefully expanded childhood illustrate the many different aspects Warsaw presented to its acculturated Jewish

---

1 Dorota Sobieska, "'Everything Comes from What I Said at the Beginning, from this Territory': An Interview with Tadeusz Konwicki," *Review of Contemporary Fiction* 14, no. 3 (Fall 1994).

residents: a picturesque, amenity-filled playground for the artistic and affluent; a generally benign society of secularized Jewish relatives, liberal Christian friends, and occasional antisemitic Poles on the street; and a wonderful school dedicated to the education of tolerant young "citizens of the world." Krystyna was spared the fate of approximately 437,000 Jews who were killed in and near Warsaw from 1940–1943—in the city streets, the Warsaw Ghetto, and the gas chambers at Treblinka. Protected by her second Warsaw family, she was fully engaged with the last stages of her prewar hometown's existence, when it served as an exciting conspiratorial underground for a Jewish teenager passing as an Aryan and represented the valiant last stand of an independent Poland. Krystyna's story as a young insurgent in the 1944 Uprising spotlights, at least in her lucky case, the lone instance when Jews and Christians fought more or less openly and *together* to free a part of Poland they loved and shared. In Warsaw, Krystyna grew up to become an intrepid Polish Jewish patriot. The Warsaw in which Krystyna lived, flourished, and fought remains the country she cherishes still. But Krystyna wisely founded her new life of family and friends in the United States, where the pluralist potential of her hometown might someday be realized.

Figure 27. Group photo of Krystyna Bierzyńska Stamper and James Stamper (seated in front row) surrounded by family members and friends. From collection of Krystyna Bierzyńska Stamper.

Works Cited

Primary source:

Interviews conducted by the author with Krystyna Bierzyńska Stamper, October 10–13, 2014, and October 23–25, 2015, at Stamper's home in Newport Beach, California. Additional interviews by phone from November 2015 through January 2017.

Secondary sources:

Białoszewski, Miron. *Memoir of the Warsaw Uprising.* Translated by Madeline G. Levine. New York: New York Review Books Classics, 2015.

Ciechanowski, Jan. M. *The Warsaw Uprising of 1944.* Cambridge: Cambridge University Press, 1974.

Grodzieńska, Stefania. *Urodził go Niebieski Ptak.* Warsaw: Wydawnictwa Radia i Telewizji, 1988.

Gutman, Yisrael. "Jews in General Anders' Army in the Soviet Union." *Yad Vashem Studies* vol. 12, Yad Vashem, Jerusalem, 1977: 231-96.

Holmgren, Beth. "Cabaret Nation: The Jewish Foundations of the Polish-Language Literary Cabaret." Forthcoming in *Polin: Studies in Polish Jewry*, Littman Library of Jewish Civilization vol. 31.

Jurandot, Jerzy. *Miasto skazanych. Dwa lata w Warszawskim getcie.* Edited by Agnieszka Arnold. Warsaw: Muzeum Historii Zydów Polskich, 2014.

Karski, Jan. *Story of a Secret State: My Report to the World.* Foreword by Madeleine Albright. Washington, DC: Georgetown University Press, 2013.

Kaufman, Haim. "Jewish Sports in the Diaspora, Yishuv, and Israel: Between Nationalism and Politics," *Israel Studies* 10, n. 2, 7/2005, 151.

"Kobiety żołnierze AK–powstańcy w niewoli niemieckiej." Edited by Maciej Janaszek-Seydlitz on the basis of reports by Witold Konecki, Stanisław Kopf, Jadwiga Kosuń Kwaśnik Badmajew, Janina Kulesza-Kurowska, Marek Ney-Krwawicz, Janina Skarzyńska, and Damian Tomczyk (2006).http://www.sppw1944.org/index.html?http://www.sppw1944.org/powstanie/kobiety_jency.html. Accessed June 12, 2017.

Korboński, Stefan. *Fighting Warsaw: The Story of the Polish Underground State, 1939–1945.* Translated by F. B. Czarnomski. Funk & Wagnalls, 1965.

Krall, Hanna. *The Subtenant: To Outwit God.* Translated by Joanna Stasinska Weschler and Lawrence Weschler. Evanston, IL: Northwestern University Press, 1992.

Krukowski, Kazimierz. *Moja Warszawka.* Warsaw: Filmowa Agencja Wydawnicza, 1957.

Moore, Deborah Dash. *GI Jews: How World War II Changed a Generation*. Cambridge: Harvard University Press, 2004.

Munk, Andrzej, dir. *Bad Luck [Zezowate Szczęście]*. 1960.

Olczak-Ronikier, Joanna. *In the Garden of Memory: A Family Memoir*. Translated by Antonia Lloyd-Jones. London: Phoenix, 2005.

Paulsson, Gunnar S. *The Secret City: The Hidden Jews of Warsaw, 1940–1945*. New Haven, CT: Yale University Press, 2002.

Person, Katarzyna. *Assimilated Jews in the Warsaw Ghetto, 1940–1943*. Syracuse: Syracuse University Press, 2014.

Polonsky, Antony. *The Jews in Russia and Poland: A Short History*. Oxford: Littman Library of Jewish Civilization, 2013.

Polonsky, Antony. *The Jews in Poland and Russia*, Vol. l. 3, *1914–2008*. Oxford: Littman Library of Jewish Civilization, 2012.

———. "The Complex Story of the Armia Krajowa" (a review of Joshua Zimmerman's *The Polish Underground and the Jews, 1939–1945*), *Yad Vashem Studies*, 43(2), 2015, 209–228.

———. "Warsaw." The Yivo Encyclopedia of Jews in Eastern Europe online. http://www.yivoencyclopedia.org/article.aspx/Warsaw. Accessed June 9, 2017.

Rosenberg, Blanca. *To Tell At Last: Survival Under False Identity, 1941–1945*. Urbana: University of Illinois Press, 1995.

Rowińska, Leokadia. *That the Nightingale Returns: Memories of the Polish Resistance, the Warsaw Uprising, and German P.O.W. Camps*. Jefferson, NC: McFarland, 1999.

Sarner, Harvey. *General Anders and the Soldiers of The Second Polish Corps*. Cathedral City, CA: Brunswick Press, 1997.

Skrzyńska, Irena. "Zarys historii kobiet-jenców wojennych żołnierzy AK internowanych po Powstaniu Warszawskim w obozie Oberlangen (stalag VlC)." http://www.polishresistance-ak.org/16%20Artykul.htm. Accessed June 12, 2017.

Sobieska, Dorota. "'Everything Comes from What I Said at the Beginning, from this Territory': An Interview with Tadeusz Konwicki." *Review of Contemporary Fiction* 14, no. 3, (Fall 1994).

Szczepańska-Wścieklica, Janka. "Pierwszy dzień wolności." *Światowy Zjazd Kobiet-Żołnierzy*, 39–40.

Światowy Zjazd Kobiet-Żołnierzy Armii Krajowej Powstania Warszawskiego, Byłych Jeńców Wojennego Obozu Oberlangen, Warsaw, April 12, 2005, 15. 60th anniversary booklet.

Terlicz-Witkowski, Leopold. "List Leopolda Terlicz-Witkowskiego." In *Światowy Zjazd Kobiet-Żołnierzy*, 20–21.

Virtual Sztetl on Tomaszów Mazowiecki. http://www.sztetl.org.pl/en/article/tomaszow-mazowiecki/3,local-history/ Accessed January 3, 2017.

Wawer, Zbigniew. *Monte Cassino 1944*. Warsaw: Bellona, 2009.

Waydenfeld, Stefan. *The Ice Road: An Epic Journey from the Stalinist Camps to Freedom*. Los Angeles: Aquila Polonica, 2011.

Załoga, S. J. *Poland 1939*. Osprey, 2002.

Zimmerman, Joshua B. *The Polish Underground and the Jews, 1939–1945*. Cambridge: Cambridge University Press, 2015.

Index

Note: Page numbers followed by 'n' denote notes

A
Academy of Fine Art, 4
akaczki, 85–87, 88n5, 89–94
Anders, Władysław, 28, 70, 100, 101
    Anders's Army (II Polish Corps), xi, 28, 91, 96, 98, 100–101, 103, 106
Anschluss, 26
Antena, 56
antisemitism, xiii, 21–22, 27, 63, 78–79, 86, 101

B
Bad Luck, 74
baptism, 28n2, 34
Barucki, Andrzej, 50
Berling, Zygmunt, 69
Białoszewski, Miron, 71, 71n8, 77, 77n12
Bierzyńska (Warmbrünn), Berta, 7, 9, 10, 19, 40, 43, 44
Bierzyńska, Krystyna, *see* Stamper (Bierzyńska), Krystyna
Bierzyńska, Maria (Marysia), 25, 39, 41, 45, 107
Bierzyńska, Regina (Rega), 25, 37, 42–44
Bierzyńska (Neufeld), Stefania, 2–4, 6, 7, 12, 13, 15, 17–23, 26–28, 30–32, 34, 37, 38–42, 44–46, 52, 103, 104
Bierzyński, Adolf (Dolek), xii, 6, 12, 13, 17–24, 27, 28, 31, 33, 46, 78, 80, 81, 91, 95, 96, 98, 99–106
Bierzyński, Beniamin (Benio), 4, 7, 8, 11–16, 18–24, 26–28, 30–34, 37, 38, 40, 45, 52, 63, 103
Bierzyński, Bernard, 6–8, 9
Bierzyński, Henryk, 6–9, 19, 25, 38, 44
Bierzyński, Jasiek, 25
Bierzyński family, 6–11
Bierzyński family portrait, 6–7
Bieżuner (Bierzyński), Natan, 7, 9–10
Blitzkrieg, 26
Bor-Komorowski, Tadeusz, 69–70
British Eighth Army, 101
Broszkowska-Piklikiewicz, Wanda, 84n1, 87n4
Brzozowska (Raczkowska), Amelia, 19, 33, 34, 49–50, 65, 67
Brzozowski, Stanisław, 19, 33
Bundists, 3, 19, 24

C
Catholicism, 5, 27–28, 34, 45, 62–63, 106
Cegalska, Marysia, 76, 84
Chapman, Eve, *acknowledgments*
Chopin, Frederic, 34, 63
Christian community, 37
Ciechanowski, Jan M., 69n3, 70
citizen of world, 20–25, 86
conspiracy, 34–36
conspiratorial identity, 1942–1944, 49–67
cosmopolitanism, 11
Cudnowa, Irena, 50, 51, 52, 55, 59, 67, 73
Częstochowa, xii, 40

D
Dmochowska, Helena, 88n5
Dolek, *see* Bierzyński, Adolf (Dolek) story, 99–103
Disney, Walt, 16

E
Edelman, Marek, 57, 68
Europejski, hotel, 14

F
Faryna, 38, 42
Fiat, car company, 14
Frank, Hans, 32
Frankiel, Tekla, 57

G
Geneva Convention, 80, 88
Genia, 21
Gennełło, Tadzio, 55, 56
Gergovich, Dr., 96–97
Gershwin, George, 60, 61, 64
Gęsia Prison, 46
Ghetto refugees, 59
Great Liquidation of summer 1942, 68
Grodzieńska, Stefania, 59, 60n5
Grossówna, Helena, 89
Gutman, Yisrael, 100n3

H
Hashomer Hatzair, 23
headstone, 37–38
Helena Modjeska Foundation, x
Hitler, Adolf, 26
Holmgren, Beth, 61n6
Home Army, 68, 69–71, 72, 73, 79, 81, 82, 90, 93, 95–107
Horwitz, Maksymilian, 13n1

I
The Information Bulletin, 68
internment
 at Oberlangen, 87–91
 at Sandbostel, 85–87
Iwo Battalion, 76

J
"Jaga." *see* Książek-Mileska, Maria Irena
Járosy, Fryderyk, 60
Jassem, Wiktor, 39
Jewish assimilation, 10
Jewish Combat Organization, 57
Jewish identity, 10–11, 28, 31, 64, 108
Jewish marriage market, 3
Jewish Military Union, 57
Jewish population in Warsaw, 9n1
Jewish self-help, 41
Jews, 2, 8, 9, 19, 22
 Hasidic Jews, 3
 Nazi campaign against, 31–34, 46, 61
 Non-Hasidic Orthodox Jews, 3
 Orthodox Jews, 7, 32, 44

Secular Jews, 3
Yiddish-speaking Jews, 31
Judaism, 9
Jurandot, Jerzy, 32, 33, 33n7, 42n4

K
Karski, Jan, 29–30, 30n4
Katyń, 50
Kaufman, Haim, 24
Kennkarte, 50
Koło, 7
Kolomyja Ghetto, 51
Konwicki, Tadeusz, 108, 109
Korboński, Stefan, 35, 35n9
Kościuszko, Tadeusz, 70
Kraków, 4, 39, 48
Krall, Hanna, 57, 57n2
Kristallnacht. 26
Krukowski, Kazimierz, 15, 15n2
Krystyna the Blue, *see* Stamper (Bierzyńska), Krystyna
Książek-Mileska, Maria Irena ("Jaga"), 88, 88n5, 89, 93
Kurier poranny, 15
Kutschera, Franz, 56, 65

L
Lardelli's, 16, 20
Łabędzka, Zofia, 50, 55, 67
liberation, 91–94
life of fugitive, 37–48
The Life of the Ant, 18
The Life of the Bee, 18
Łódź, 3
Lwów, 47, 48
Lycée Français de Varsovie, 23, 24, 25

M
Maczek, Stanisław, 91, 94, 95
Maeterlinck, Maurice, 18
Marczewska, Janina (Nina), 2, 3, 4, 19, 27, 42, 43, 46, 48, 49, 50, 55, 59
Marczewska, Maria (Marysia), 2, 54–55, 59
A Midsummer Night's Dream, 16, 30
Modjeska, Helena, x, xi
Molotov-Ribbentrop Pact, 26, 28, 99, 100
Monte Cassino (battle), 102–103, 105
Monte Cassino 1944, 102
Mortkowicz, Jakub, 10
multiculturalism, 105
Munk, Andrzej, 74
muscular Jewry, 24

N

National Democrats (Endecja), 13, 101
Nazis, 2, 26, 51, 61, 79, 85, 105
    campaign against the Jews, 31–34
Neufeld (Landau), Gustawa, 2, 3, 5, 7, 108
Niederlangen, internment, 94, 98

O

Oberlangen, internment, 84, 87–91, 95, 107
Olczak-Ronikier, Joanna, 10, 10n2, 13n1
Olek, 60, 61, 63, 64
Omega Maternity Hospital, 13
Orange County, inland wilderness, x

P

Paulsson, Gunnar S., 39n1, 41
Pawiak Prison, 49
Piłsudski, Marshal Józef, 13, 14, 21, 22, 34, 63
Plater, Emilia, 22
Podłęże, 44
Poland, 1
    Moscow-allied government, 1
    partitions, 35
    Second Republic of, 13
Polish American heritage, x
Polish bandits, 61
Polish Catholic heroism, 105
Polish Committee of National Liberation (PKWN), 69
Polish prisoners of war, 1944–1945, 86, 84–94, 104, 108
Polish Resistance, 35, 63, 64
Polonisation, 10
of Jewish surnames, 8
Polonsky, Antony, 13n1, 32n5, 82n18, 100n1
Pospiszel, Dagmar, 23
powstaniec, 82

R

Raczkowska, Barbara (Basia), 52, 53–56, 66–67, 80, 81, 91
Raczkowska, Zofia, 49, 50, 52, 59, 67
Ravensbrück, 59
Reymont, Władysław, 34
Rhapsody in Blue, 60, 64
Rosenberg, Blanca, 51, 51n1, 59
Rowińska, Leokadia, 62, 62n7, 71, 81
Royal Palace, Warsaw, 29
Różycki, Dr., 102

S

Salamucha, Father Jan, 73
Sandbostel, internment, 85–87
Santa Ana, California, x
Sarner, Harvey, 100, 101n4, 102, 102n5
Skrzyńska, Irena, 93
Snow White and the Seven Dwarves (1937), 16
Sobieska, Dorota, 109, 109n1
Sorbonne University, 22
Soviet Union, 28, 101
Stalin, Joseph, xi, 69, 80
Stamper, James, x, 110
Stamper (Bierzyńska), Krystyna, x, xi, xii, 1, 2, 4, 5, 9, 11–13, 15–22, 24–28, 30–34, 38, 39, 41–49, 51, 52, 54, 56–59, 61–63, 65–68, 71–74, 82, 84, 86, 110
    conspirator, 54–57
    family pact, 95–106
    Jewish in 1944 uprising, 78–83
    joins 1944 uprising, 74–78
    new family council, 49–54
    Oberlangen, internment, 87–91
    in Polish history, 107–110
    Sandbostel, internment, 85–87
    story, 103–106
Stasia, 16–17, 31
Sthęka, Grażyna, *acknowledgments*, 54
Stęcka (Bierzyńska) Matylda, 7, 54
Stęcki, Henryk, 7
Stroop, Jürgen, 58
Sylwester, 56
Szczepańska-Wścieklica, Janka, 93
Światowy Zjazd Kobiet-Żołnierzy, 88n5
Świder, 65–67

T

Tatras, 24, 65
Ter Apel, 92
Terlicz-Witkowski, Leopold, 91, 92–93
Tomaszów Mazowiecki, 3, 4, 9, 27
Treblinka, 46, 110

U

Umschlagplatz, 46, 71–72

V

Virtuti Militari, 103, 104, 107

W

Wanda Szachtmajerowa High School, 34–36, 55, 63

Warsaw
- before the War (1928–1939), 11, 12–19
- bombardment of, 29–31
- conspiratorial activities during the war, 1942–1944, 49–67
- everyday terror in, 61–67
- interwar period, 16
- invasion and occupation, 1939–1940, 26–36
- Krystyna's flight to, 47–48
- living conditions, 20, 51–52
- parks, 16
- Saxon Gardens, 16, 20, 21, 30
- theaters, 15–16, 30

Warsaw Gestapo, 56
Warsaw Ghetto, xi–xii, 32, 33, 40, 41, 42, 45–46, 72
- 1943 Warsaw Ghetto Uprising, 3, 52, 57–61, 68–69, 74, 79, 104

1944 Warsaw Uprising, x, xi, 1, 4, 59, 62, 64, 68–83, 109
- Attack on insurgents, 73

Warszawska (Neufeld), Janina (Nina), 2–4, 33, 40, 42, 43
Warszawska, Wanda, 42, 43, 52
Warszawski, Fabian, 4, 27, 43
Wawer, Zbigniew, 102, 103n6
Waydenfeld, Stefan, 100, 100n2
Wiadomości literackie, 15
Wilek, 27, 48
World War I, 8
World War II, 35, 82, 109
Wysocka, Alla, 55, 56

Z

Zabierzów, 1, 8, 25, 26, 37, 38, 40, 42, 44, 45, 52
- German roundup in, 42–46

Zachęta National Art Gallery, 15, 17
Zacieniuk, Stefan, 52–54, 56, 65, 80, 81, 91
Zakopane, 25
Ziemiańska Café, 15
Zimmerman, Joshua B., 68n1, 69, 72, 78
Zionists, 3, 19, 20–21, 23, 24
Zionist-socialist youth movement, 23
Zośka Battalion, 77–78
Zylber, Adolf, 3, 4, 8, 31, 40
Zylber (Neufeld), Aniela, 3, 19, 31, 33, 40, 42, 45–48

www.ingramcontent.com/pod-product-compliance
Lightning Source LLC
Chambersburg PA
CBHW070939180426
43192CB00039B/2340